Beginners Guide to Building

Ecommerce

Websites With Wordpress and Elementor

Easy Steps to Build and Launch Ecommence Websites for Dropshipping and

Online Businesses

TED

HUMPHREY

Copyright

Contents

Copyright i

Chapter One 1

Introduction to E-commerce Websites 1

What is e-commerce? 1

Differences between e-commerce and e-business 2

Advantages and disadvantages of creating an e-commerce 5

Steps to create an e-commerce 7

Characteristics of an E-commerce Website 10

History of E-commerce and E-commerce Websites 13

Everything was born from the sale by catalog 13

The first credit card 14

The real start of an e-commerce 14

Electronic modernization of the catalog 15

The Internet came to adopt it all 15

Creation of the WWW 15

The future of e-commerce 16

Types of E-commerce Websites 16

B2B electronic commerce 17

B2C e-commerce 17

E-commerce P2P 17

C2C electronic commerce 18

G2C e-commerce 18

B2G E-commerce 18

E-commerce B2E 19

Chapter Two 20

Choosing a Domain Name and Hosting 20

Choosing a Domain Name 20

What Is A Domain Name 20

What is the difference between a domain name and a web host? 20

Why are domain names important? 21

How much does a domain name cost? 21

How to choose the right domain extension? 22

How do I find the right domain name? 22

Important points for choosing a domain name 27

The 5 best registrars for 2020 30

Chapter Three 35

Installing WordPress and Account Setup through Control Panel 35

A Step-by-step Guide on how to Install WordPress and Continue with Building
of your Website 36

Installing a New Theme and Plugins On WordPress 39

Install a paid WordPress theme (Pro/Premium version) 39

Configure your WordPress theme 40

Step-by-Step Guide in Installing Plug-ins 41

Where to find WordPress plugins (extensions)? 41

Install a free plugin from the WordPress directory 43

Common Bugs You May experience after installing your website 43

WooCommerce Plug-in 49

Install and configure the Woocommerce plugin on your WordPress site....................51

Creating the structure of your WooCommerce online store 52

Configure your WooCommerce store settings 54

The configuration of automatic emails sent to your customers 55

Creating the product pages for your WooCommerce site...56

Chapter Four..58

Setting Up WooCommerce Payment Methods 58

Setting up a sandbox account with PayPal and creating users 60

API credential Section in Setting up PayPal Payment Account (Sandbox Account) to receive Payments..61

PayPal Account setup..61

API Access Live PayPal account 61

Setting up Payment Gateway for Ecommerce Websites in India...............................62

How to Install Instamojo Plugin on WordPress 63

How to get API Credentials Information from Instamojo to setup Payments Method with WooCommerce...63

Setting up Pages and adding them as Menu Items..65

Create the product pages for your WooCommerce site...66

Add Your First Product 67

Chapter Five 68

Designing E-Commerce Webpages with Elementor and the Design of other Sections 68

Why and when to create custom layouts in WordPress? 68

Getting Started with Elementor 69

Creating a custom layout with Elementor 70

Chapter Six 75

How to Market and Promote your E-Commerce Store 75

Paid SEO: Online advertising for your e-commerce site 76

The impact of Social Media Sites on Promotion of Online Stores 78

How to Advertise your E-Commerce Site with Google Shopping (Google Ads) 79

How does Google Shopping work? 81

Creating an account on Google Merchant Center 82

Link Google Merchant Center to AdWords 87

Creating ads on AdWords and set the budget 88

How to Advertise your E-commerce site on Facebook 89

Advertising your Store through Radio and Television Channels 91

About Author 95

Chapter One

Introduction to E-commerce Websites

It is quite likely because e-commerce is all the rage now more than ever. However, like many, you may not know the exact meaning of this term, nor the differences between e-commerce and other related concepts.

The objective of this book is to give you a precise definition of e-commerce websites and to explain how it differs from other similar concepts. We'll also go over the different types of e-commerce, as well as the advantages of e-commerce over traditional commerce.

Are you ready to find out everything you need to know about e-commerce websites? Let's go!

What is e-commerce?

According to Wikipedia, e-commerce, or electronic commerce, is... "The monetary exchange of goods, services, and information via computer networks, in particular, the Internet". In other words, it is a business that handles payments through electronic means. An e-commerce site, also called a merchant site, is an Internet site whose main activity is to do online commerce (sell/buy via the Internet). It, therefore, designates anything relating to an exchange of goods and services between companies and individuals on the Internet. A branch of e-business, the e-commerce site can be broken down into different types of electronic commerce:

A B2C (Business to Consumer) site: concerns an e-commerce site between a company and its customers (Internet users).

A B2B (Business to Business) site: describes an e-commerce site between companies (a company sells to other companies).

A B2E (Business to Employee) site: refers to the e-commerce site of a company for its employees.

A B2G (Business to Government) site: qualifies the e-commerce site between a company and local authorities (a company sells to a public company, for example).

Unlike e-business, which covers the very wide use of the Internet tool to optimize an exchange of information, the e-commerce site focuses only on the purchasing process. Thus, this type of site allows customers to create accounts, add products (items) to their cart, adjust their shipping costs, choose their payment method, track their order, etc.

To offer the best shopping experience to customers, an e-commerce site guarantees a secure payment system and generally offers a detailed catalog of products and/or services sold. Other pages are also essential:

- Home page
- A site map
- A page containing the legal notices and the general conditions of sale
- A basket of orders
- A contact form

Differences between e-commerce and e-business

E-commerce and e-business are two concepts that we tend to confuse. In reality, they have nothing to do with each other.

E-commerce only refers to the transaction of goods and services between a buyer and a seller. E-business, on the other hand, refers to the entire process to be implemented to manage an online business.

Inside e-business, we find for example (links in English):

- The inbound marketing
- the promotions
- The stock management

- the SEO
- The email marketing
- etc.

As we can see, the concept of e-business is much broader than that of e-commerce. As a type of business model, e-commerce is part of e-business. The world of e-commerce is very large and includes several distinct models. It is possible to make 2 classifications:

- A global classification based on the business model (who sells and who buys)
- Another based on the business model.

Let's go.

1. According to the commercial profile

Each trade is aimed at a specific type of customer. This allows us to distinguish the following types of e-commerce:

B2B (Business-to-Business): companies whose end customers are other companies or other organizations. For example, a building material store that caters to architects or interior designers.

B2C (Business-to-Consumer): companies that sell products or services directly to end consumers. This is the most common form, and there is a multitude of examples in the fields of fashion, electronics, etc.

C2B (Consumer-to-Business): portals on which consumers offer a product or service that companies can acquire. These are the classic freelance job portals like Elance, Odesk, Humaniance, Upwork, etc.

C2C (Consumer-to-Consumer): companies that facilitate the sale of products between consumers. The most telling examples are eBay, Leboncoin, or any portal for the sale of second-hand items between individuals.

These forms of electronic commerce are the most common. There are also other types, such as G2C (Government-to-Consumer), C2G (Consumer- to-Government), or B2E Business-to-Employer). As we can see, e-commerce brings together realities that go beyond a simple purchase in a store.

2. Depending on the business model

The online world is still a little mature sector. Technological changes are constant and new online businesses meet new needs. We can differentiate the type of e-commerce according to the income generated or how the exchange takes place between the buyer and the seller:

- Online store with its products: This is the first thing you think of when you think of e-commerce. The same characteristics as a physical store, in an online version.
- Dropshipping: To the customer, it appears to be normal e-commerce. The difference is that it is a third party who sends the product, not the seller. To learn more about dropshipping, we advise you to read our complete guide dedicated to dropshipping (in French).
- Affiliate e-commerce: Affiliate businesses go even further than drop shipping. In this case, not only does the store not send the product, but the sale does not take place on its platform. The e-commerce redirects the customer to another store, which pays him a commission once the sale is concluded. Affiliation with Amazon is the most common. For example Biodegradable.es. If you are interested in these models, do not hesitate to read our articles (in English) devoted specifically to affiliate marketing or even selling without stock.
- Membership: This type of e-commerce seeks its customers to make recurring purchases. The preferred way to obtain them is through a periodic subscription (weekly, monthly, quarterly, etc.). This type of membership is currently in vogue with "surprise boxes". This is a box sent monthly (or at another frequency) and contains certain products. One of our customers, NUOObox, offers, for example, boxes of natural and organic cosmetics. The advantage of this model is to ensure a recurring income each month.
- Marketplace: A marketplace is a store grouping together several stores. This is a website where different sellers offer their products. Amazon is the

example of a marketplace par excellence: several companies put their products for sale on the platform in exchange for a commission paid to Amazon.

- Services: E-commerce does not necessarily sell products. Training, advice, coaching, and, in general, any time exchanged for money. This is a good viable option to start without taking any risks.

As we have seen previously, advances in this sector are daily, and new types of electronic commerce are constantly emerging.

Advantages and disadvantages of creating an e-commerce

Why has e-commerce become so numerous on the Internet in such a short time? First, because e-commerce represents significant advantages over traditional commerce let us see which ones.

Benefits

More customers: Neither a local store nor a company established in several cities can reach as many people as e-commerce. Being able to buy and sell from anywhere in the world greatly expands the target audience and leads to more customers.

No hours: unlike traditional shops, which are rarely open 24 hours a day, e-commerce has no hours. The website remains open and accessible to the public all day, so the customer can shop at any time.

Lower costs: being able to do without a physical establishment reduces costs compared to the operation of a traditional business. And if e-commerce works by putting suppliers in contact with buyers, there will not even be production costs (in the case of dropshipping, which we were talking about above).

More margin: The reduction in costs and the increase in the number of customers make it possible to achieve a greater margin than with traditional trade, even at lower prices. We sell more and we earn more money.

Scalability: In e-commerce, you can sell to one or a thousand people at the same time. In a physical business, there is always a limit to the number of clients you can serve at a time; in e-commerce, the limit is your ability to attract visitors. And of course, that of your computer server. ;)

Reading all of these benefits, you might think that starting e-commerce is the panacea. However, we must be aware of the difficulties that e-commerce can represent.

It is therefore necessary to analyze the challenges you will face when you start your online adventure.

Disadvantages / challenges

We prefer to talk about challenges than inconveniences so as not to distort reality.

Certain disadvantages exist, of course (as with everything in life!) However, without them, starting an online business would be too easy and lose its value.)

1. Lack of Confidence: Although gateways and payment methods have come a long way and are today as secure as in physical stores, many people continue to not fully trust online transactions. To help them to trust more, it is possible to use an SSL certificate (https) which encrypts the transferred information, as well as other certificates, which make it possible to guarantee the security of the client.

2. Products and services that cannot be seen or touched: As customers, we like to feel like we are making a good purchase. We like to see the product and touch it to realize its quality and this cannot be done in e-commerce. How to overcome this drawback? Thanks to comprehensive product sheets, including images, videos, and a very detailed description of the product.

3. Internet connection essential: It is obvious, but to sell and buy on the Internet, a device connected to the Internet is necessary. This does not apply to the majority of online activities, but maybe a problem for some industries where the target audience is older or less familiar with new technologies.

4. Technical difficulties: Dealing with unknown themes is the daily life of entrepreneurs, whether offline or online. In the case of e-commerce, the technological part requires a minimum of technological knowledge, which not everyone has. The best way to solve this difficulty is to delegate this part, although this comes at a cost.

5. Competition: The economic entry barrier to creating e-commerce is not as high as for a physical store. The competition is, therefore, more important, and you have to be more competent than the others.

6. Time to get results: When a brick-and-mortar store opens, customers walking past see it. Getting visibility for an online business is harder than it looks. Indeed, you can have a great product and be present on a good platform, but if you don't work to gain visibility, no one will notice you.

Steps to create an e-commerce

Now that you know what e-commerce is and the pros and cons, let's see where to start.

1. The idea

Do you already have an idea or are you starting from scratch? If you are not yet sure, there are several techniques you can use to spot opportunities.

All are based on open-mindedness and a good sense of observation. It is about seeing everyday situations through the eye of the entrepreneur.

When you walk down the street, watch out for physical businesses that could transpose onto the Internet, if they haven't already.

Think about your needs and those of the people around you: what do they use every day? What are they complaining about?

Go out on the streets explicitly in search of ideas

Look at what people you meet are wearing, the way they behave. Observe and write down every idea that comes to your mind, without filtering them.

Think over and over again how you could solve the problems of the people you meet. Your entrepreneurial spirit is like a muscle you need to train: when you start going to the gym you will feel aches and pains for the first few days, but as you go, your body gets used to the exercises. It works the same way. But the most important thing is to put this idea in your head: don't sell products, solve problems.

2. Analysis of the idea

The second step is to sort through the initial ideas until you have just one or a few left.

It will be this idea of e-commerce that we are going to analyze.

- Value proposition: what is the value provided? What need does the idea satisfy?
- Market: is it a new product? A product that already exists, but which offers new features?
- Competition: currently, who is meeting the need you have identified? Could you improve the product or service?
- Demand: Is the problem you are going to solve large enough to generate a great demand? Check how many Google searches exist for the topic. You can do this with Keyword Planner.
- Difficulties: list other challenges that come to mind (technical difficulties, competition, threats, etc.)

A great way to analyze an idea is to do it with a basic entrepreneurial tool: the SWOT.

S = Strengths (forces), W = Weaknesses (weaknesses), O = Opportunities (opportunities), T = threats (threats)

SWOT analysis is a business strategy tool that allows you to analyze from an internal and external point of view the strengths, weaknesses, opportunities, and threats of your idea.

3. Strategy

According to INSEE, more than 500 companies are created in some countries every day, but the majority are without having defined a strategy in advance.

And be convinced that knowing the direction to take and the means to get there will be the key to your success.

You can ask yourself questions like:

- How will our ideal client get to know us?
- Why are we going to be preferred to the competition?
- Are we going to be cheap?
- What defines our customers? What common characteristics do they share?
- What are the objectives of our business? How are we going to grow up?

To define the e-commerce strategy, we will use the Business Model Canvas.

This model simply and quickly summarizes the keys to a business. Spending time filling in these nine boxes will help you identify what is important to your idea and how to make it happen.

4. Action plan

So far, you have defined general ideas and goals. In this fourth part, we will deal more concretely with specific actions.

Here are some ideas:

- Name: This is one of the puzzles at the start. Our advice is to follow basic rules: a short name, easy to pronounce, available in the.com domain, and on the main social networks.
- Hosting: Electronic commerce requires to be hosted by a server. Don't worry, we've written an article where we explain how to choose to host for your e-commerce.
- Corporate identity: Here we are not only talking about the colors or the logo, but the values to be transmitted, the true essence of the brand. Do not hesitate to read our post in which we explain how to create your brand image.
- Website: who will build the website? If you don't do it yourself, you'll need someone to do it for you and who can advise you. Consider the different options available to you depending on your business model: PrestaShop, WordPress, Shopify, etc.
- Visibility: This is the last point, but it's the most important and most overlooked part. The majority of entrepreneurs strive for a good product and a beautiful website to sell it, but they forget to think about how customers will arrive.

Finally, you should not neglect the legal issues. Are you going to set up an LLC? Are you going to register as a self-employed person?

Characteristics of an E-commerce Website

E-commerce or electronic commerce is extremely popular today, given the ease and speed of acquiring products and services on the internet. Although most e-commerce is managed on social networks, many brands and companies have websites that facilitate and encourage the purchase of their goods. E-commerce can be safe if the seller and the product have recognition or endorsement from other users or consumers, because unlike traditional purchases, in e-commerce you can only see the product through photos or videos. E-commerce not only sells goods and products, but some companies sell services, which further complicates the generation of user trust.

E-commerce is presented as a possibility to diversify the sales of a brand. There are a wide variety of platforms that facilitate the creation of a virtual store such as Open Source, on the other hand, SaaS, whether they are free or paid software, offer their products through social networks instead of using a site Web. Given the diversity that exists for the creation of a platform that facilitates the sale of products or services of a company, we offer you the 5 main characteristics of e-commerce so that at the time of its development you can do it successfully:

Ease of navigation:

The main thing is that the user can quickly find and access the product they are looking for, the fewer clicks they have to do on the site, the better. Intuitive and assertive navigation is essential for e-commerce since it translates into the reduction of lost sales.

The products must be highlighted before the site design:

Although an attractive site can be a plus, we generally tend to think that they will attract more users. For e-commerce, the main thing is quick access to products, they must stand out and provide the most information in this regard to generate sufficient trust. You can use photographs or even videos that try to realistically show the product in question.

Display the best selling or popular products:

If e-commerce has a wide variety of products to sell, the user may get lost in that search. One way to attract more attention is to place or group the best-selling items by category.

Product photos in detail:

As we indicated previously, the photographs and any other content that you share concerning the product is very important, especially to generate trust with the user and to demonstrate quality.

Facilitate the purchase process:

E-commerce is based on the shopping experience. The faster and safer they are, the better for the user to buy back. The purchase process should be short and simple so that the user does not lose interest and leave the site.

Some examples of an e-commerce site

Amazon.com

Founded in 1994 in Seattle by the now immortal Jeff Bezos, Amazon has since become a household name in the online shopping world. This internet company has the largest turnover in the world today, but its beginnings were small. Initially, it was just an online bookstore, diversifying the range of products it sold online over the following years. Who says books can't pay off!

jd.com

His name is Jingdong.

This e-commerce company operating out of Beijing is the first of the three big Chinese companies that we list here. Rivaled by the most popular Alibaba, Jingdong has well over a quarter of a billion registered users as of 2018. It was founded in 1998 and began trading online six years later. Today, the company wields its high-tech delivery system, made up of robots, AI, and a fleet of drones. They are so crazy about technology that they have plans to build drone airports, flying training, and even flight control for drones that deliver cargo. They teamed up with scientists to design drones that could carry cargo weighing up to a metric ton!

Zalando.de

Surprisingly, this is the first European company that we list. Zalando's head office is in Berlin and they mainly have online stores that sell fashion items, such as clothes and shoes. Their logo looks like an orange guitar pick.

History of E-commerce and E-commerce Websites

In this context, we have compiled the most important things about the history of electronic commerce, its evolution in Latin America, and what the future of this sector promises. The beginnings of the history of electronic commerce go back to times that you can't imagine. What you see today as a virtual store is the latest evolution of a long line of innovations and development.

And, for all those who are part of the industry and who consume it, it is essential to understand where it comes from, to visualize what it can become in the future. You likely think that the history of electronic commerce is closely associated with the Internet. Today this is a reality, but in the beginning, it was not.

Everything was born from the sale by catalog

Sure you did not imagine it, but the first step that was taken for what we know today as e-commerce, on the planet, was sales by catalogs in the 20s and 30s of the 20th century in the United States. This business model broke with everything established because it allowed consumers to order their favorite products without leaving home.

Here the industry realized that the consumer wanted to buy, but with the comfort of avoiding going to a physical store and taking the products home.

The phone was no longer just for talking to loved ones

Catalog sales evolved thanks to the expansion of the phone throughout the United States. And what was used as a means of communication with family and friends became the vendors' master tool. Telephone orders changed the business model of many companies since they could understand that there was a real and abundant market in this sector and that traditional methods were not the only way to make money.

The first credit card

In 1914 the money transfer company, Western Union, launched this financial tool on the market.

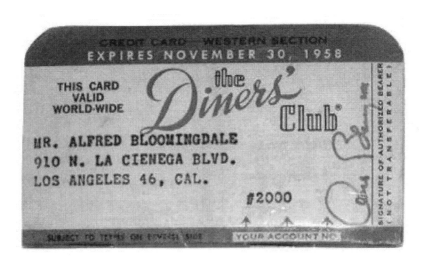

But it was not until the 1950s, with the popularity of telephone purchases, that the public realized its value and usefulness since you did not have to be present or have physical money to pay for their products and services.

The real start of an e-commerce

In 1960, a tool was invented that would change everything. The Electronic Data Interchange or EDI, a platform that made it easier for companies to transmit financial data electronically, such as purchase orders and invoices. This stage was essential for catalog and telephone sales thanks to the rise of telesales. Where, between television shows, product demos were shown and consumers were allowed to call to order these products and pay for them with credit cards.

Electronic modernization of the catalog

In the late 1970s, Michael Aldrich of England created a revolutionary concept, which involved connecting a modified home television via telephone to a multi-user computerized processing line. In other words, he managed to make the first electronic sales computer transactions. Its technology was applied in countries such as Ireland, Spain, and the United Kingdom in the first B2B (Business to Business) financial transfers, where companies could buy and sell tour packages, rent, sell and buy cars, make money loans, access credit history, among others.

The Internet came to adopt it all

At this time, computers had not yet appeared as such. It was not until the 1970s that the first commercial relationships appeared that used a computer, but still offered a very limited service. It was not until 1980 that catalog commerce was modernized with the help of television with " telesales ". Television provided catalog commerce with a greater realism of the products since they could be exhibited highlighting their most important attributes and characteristics. This type of direct sales was made through the use of telephone calls and payment was made through credit cards.

Creation of the WWW

1989 was a watershed year for technology and later for e-commerce as well. A new star service appeared and it turned out to be the most important innovation, the WWW, or World Wide Web. The website was created by Englishman Tim Berners-Lee while working at CERN in Geneva, Switzerland. This method of transmitting information between computers would completely change the way of communicating and also of marketing. The message from Tim Berners-Lee the inventor of the WWW at the London 2012 Olympics.

In the late 1990s, with the Internetworking, e-commerce grew like never before. Portals exclusively dedicated to this activity were created - such as eBay and Amazon, which remain operational and growing until today. The last step to consolidate electronic commerce as we understand it was in 1995 when the members of the G7 / G8 created the initiative of a global market for SMEs. This platform had the objective of increasing the use of E-commerce among companies around the world, and it worked.

The future of e-commerce

Social networks, mobile communications, web 2.0., Smartphones, tablets that we have within our reach today are changing the consumption habits of our world. It is no longer enough to put a catalog of products in an online store in a static way and wait for users to buy. More and more people are using their tablets or smartphones to carry out searches, compare prices, and also to buy online. This trend will prevail in the not too distant future and companies that want to sell online will have to adapt to these new habits and devices. What we can see is that the history of electronic commerce began thanks to the fact that innovators realized that the consumer needs simpler and more comfortable purchasing methods. In this sense, sales and marketing models were created that would bring stores to homes and offices, and innovations such as voice-commerce today.

Types of E-commerce Websites

There are various actors to consider in this type of trade. Commonly, the different types of models are linked to the acronyms of the actors they refer to. These actors are the company (B), the consumers (C), the administration (G), the investors (I), and the employees (E).

Technology is there to make life easier for us in all aspects and in business, it could not be different. Any person or brand can sell and buy without the need to have a physical business. An Internet connection is sufficient to accomplish this task. The most outstanding classification of the different types of electronic commerce is as follows:

B2B electronic commerce

B2B means Business to Business. As its name implies, it is the type of business in which commercial operations are carried out between companies with an Internet presence. Here the audience or the consuming public does not intervene, the operations focus on sellers, suppliers, buyers, and intermediaries. In this type of trade, sellers seek buyers, buyers seek suppliers, or intermediaries enter into commercial agreements between sellers and buyers. As we can see, B2B electronic commerce fosters, above all, commercial relationships between companies.

B2C e-commerce

B2C means Business to Consumer, in Spanish it is Business to Consumer. It is one that is carried out through virtual sites, in which the public acquires a product or service from the company of their interest. It focuses on the well-known online stores that have the ease of quick access at any time and place for the consumer who is connected to the Internet.

On the other hand, businesses or companies can provide better customer service since they can interact with consumers directly through various platforms and social networks. Not to mention that they can update relevant information constantly. This kind of commerce encourages the appearance of intermediaries, companies that are dedicated to facilitating purchases between customers, and various virtual stores in exchange for a commission or fixed payment.

E-commerce P2P

P2P, Peer to Peer Network is the model in which consumers exchange information. Here the trade is created and managed by users who sell their products directly to other people. Users need a platform to put an order in the agreements and transactions of the operators. These platforms take a commission for this kind of service. Great examples of this we find in Zilok, and Airbnb.

C2C electronic commerce

C2C or Consumer to Consumer. It is the type of trade in which people who no longer use an object seek to sell it to other people, operating of course on platforms connected to the Internet. The neighborhood markets or garage sales have been transported to the digital world. Here the consuming public exercises commercial operations among itself.

Items that are no longer needed are sold at very affordable prices, thus promoting the reuse of products, purchases at a lower cost and a much greater scope than could be had in a neighborhood street market. For example, consider social media pages made for this purpose or platforms such as Segunda Mano.

G2C e-commerce

The acronyms of this type of business mean Government to Consumer or, from the Government to the Consumer. The digital governments of certain countries have taken advantage of online trading. Let's think about the facilities that governments grant for citizens to carry out their procedures and payments through some digital platform. This is commerce since you pay for a document or service and because you can access the online platform at any time. With this type of transaction, both citizens and public officials save time and money, have electronic backups and the procedures are much more secure.

B2G E-commerce

The abbreviation B2G stands for Business to Government. As the name implies, this type of electronic commerce focuses on negotiation processes between companies and the government through digital technology or the Internet. Its action is exercised in digital portals that have to do with public administration, through these, government organizations contact companies for the acquisition of products or services. This even helps government organizations charged with administration save money and time through simple product purchasing or order picking processes. B2G is the type of electronic commerce in which companies specialized in marketing, engineering projects, or, well, consultancy providers, can promote themselves.

E-commerce B2E

The acronym for this type of business means Business to Employee. As the name implies, it focuses on the business relationship between a company and its workers. His focus is to promote offers to his employees from his online store, based on striking proposals that serve to create a better job performance.

It is also common that in these online sites, in addition to shopping as an incentive, workers carry out procedures that will reach the indicated departments much more efficiently. In this way companies reduce costs in internal activities, internal e-commerce is created, workers are motivated and the website can be used as a way of consulting. The variety of types of electronic commerce allows anyone to start a business online. It is only necessary to choose one of the types of electronic commerce that exists and gets to work!

Chapter Two

Choosing a Domain Name and Hosting

Choosing a Domain Name

If you are thinking of looking for a domain name, you should know that the adventure is not as easy as you might think. Does it sound good? Does it limit the type of products you can sell? Is it a brand name or are they keywords? How do consumers react when they hear your domain name? Also, it is not enough to choose a domain name, it is also necessary that you can buy it. With over 1.90 billion websites, there's a good chance that the domain name you want has already been taken. But don't worry, this section guides you through this exciting adventure. After all, if you're looking for a domain name, it's good that you're about to launch your site.

We will see together how to find an available and effective domain name and how to verify a domain name. I also tell you where to find free domain names or how to buy them.

What Is a Domain Name

This is the address or URL that people type into their search engine to reach your website. When this address is entered in the search bar, it causes a query to your web host, which "grabs" your site and displays it on the requester's browser. Here are some examples of domain names: Google.com, Facebook.com, and Twitter.com

What is the difference between a domain name and a web host?

As its name suggests, the host hosts your website and the domain name to which it is attached. Several companies offer both domain registration and hosting services to make it easier to launch a website. That said, nothing is stopping you from using two different companies.

Why are domain names important?

A domain name is essential because it allows you to develop a brand that brings together an audience, it helps consumers find you online and gives you credibility. While the success of a website depends on other factors, owning a domain has several advantages:

Visibility: If your business is not online, it does not exist. If you own a physical store in a remote town that no one knows about, you'll exist even less online. But if you build a website around your brand, you gain visibility, especially if you optimize your site name for search engines.

Credibility: While having a URL isn't everything, running your website gives your brand more credibility. If you start a small business without having an official website, a lot of consumers may not trust you. However, trust is essential in e-commerce and customers always turn to sites that they can easily find, whose content they can see, for which they find opinions, etc. Having a website is the first step in building credibility online.

A brand: A good domain name gives authenticity to your brand, especially if it matches your business name. It also allows your brand to gain a reputation more quickly because people remember your business name and will talk about it around them. When buying a name, make sure it is easy to remember and that it accurately represents your brand.

How much does a domain name cost?

For most domain names with a simple extension such as .fr or .com, you shouldn't pay more than $10 or $20 per year. Newer extensions such as .me, .app, .health, .photo, etc, are more expensive because these rates are negotiated between registrars (companies that sell domain names) and ICANN (Internet Corporation for Assigned Names and Numbers). It is important to emphasize that a domain cannot be bought for life. You will need to renew it every year and pay a slightly higher price than what you paid when registering. The reason is that registrars offer promotions to new customers. You will also have additional costs if you add any options to this service, such as data protection, a personalized email address, or automatic backups.

How to choose the right domain extension?

With all of the extension options available, how do you choose the right one for your business? The simplest choice remains.com if it is available. It is indeed the extension having the most value and the most used. According to The GrowthBadger Blog, this extension is 33% easier to remember than any other domain extension. If that is not possible either, then fall back on the.org (usually reserved for organizations of all kinds) or on the.net. Finally, it makes perfect sense and smart to choose a.fr extension if your business is based in France.

You can also look to more creative options. For example .bio if you offer natural products or .store to make your online store stand out immediately. It doesn't matter whether you have an online store or a physical store, that little difference can make a big difference in growing your business.

How do I find the right domain name?

When thinking about your future name, there are several important things to consider. Here are some tips for finding a domain name for your brand:

1. Find your niche

If some domain names are free, maybe they are for the wrong reasons. For example, it is possible to find a very good domain name available, because it was penalized by Google during the time of its previous owner. It will take a long time to get out of the penalty and be well referenced again. Don't fall for this trap. This can seriously hinder you from developing your brand. If you have already invested, you can verify a domain name and see if it has already been penalized using tools like https://ismywebsitepenalized.com/. Duplicate content, content farms, or low quality and volume content are among the reasons that can lead a site to be penalized.

Another reason why a domain name could be a bad investment is related to an unpopular niche or one that has too low volumes of requests. In this case, no matter how hard you scramble, it will be very difficult for you to attract traffic to your site.

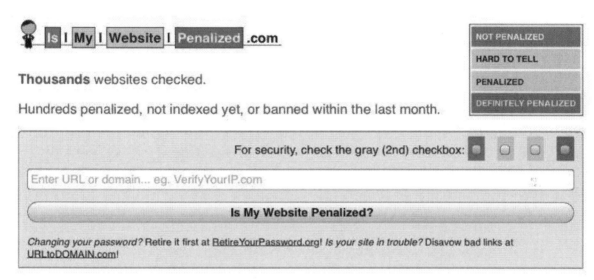

FREQUENTLY-ASKED-QUESTIONS

What is IsMyWebsitePenalized.com (IMWP)?

IMWP is a free service for webmasters, website owners, and SEO professionals. Our goal is simple - to perform a quick and secure search engine penalty test and give you a clear answer about whether or not your website is penalized by Google search engine.

2. Check the availability of a site

You can use sites like WHOIS to verify a domain name. Type in the name you're interested in and you'll see right away if it already belongs to someone. Be careful, you will find some domain names available but at exorbitant prices, because their owners want to sell them. If the name you are interested in is already taken, it is better to look for another right away. Indeed, it is useless to compete with an already existing site. By the way, this name is probably copyrighted and you might get into trouble with the law if you use it. For these reasons, I recommend that you do not persevere in adding words such as a boutique, store, or any other term that would allow you to use that name.

HOSTING SERVICES

Trust your site to one of the Largest Hosting Providers to Small Businesses

3. Search first, buy next

Sure, you'll do better to act fast if the domain name you love is available, but don't rush either. I bought several domain names myself that I have never used because I realized after the fact that they were better. Or that my business was taking a different direction. I'm in a good position to know that enthusiasm can go down as quickly as it goes up. If you have a good idea for a domain name, do some research right away. What is the request volume for these terms? For your niche? Is this brand name appropriate? Is it easy to read? Once you have done your research carefully and are sure this name accurately represents your branding, then buy it. If your niche is in a strong development phase, you have to act quickly. Just make sure this is the case before you take out your payment card.

4. Check the copyrights before purchasing

You should also check the licenses for that domain name before purchasing it. One day, I bought a domain name that I loved and the idea of using it for my new brand excited me the most. Until I discussed it with a friend who said to me: "I am surprised that this name is not registered". I did some research: it was well deposited. So I had spent some money on a domain that I couldn't use. When doing your research for your domain name, do a search engine query with the name in question and the term "registered". Common expressions or names close to existing brands may be registered trademarks. If you find an available and great domain name, now is the time to do this research.

5. Buy it when you find it

Once you've found the perfect domain name and done your homework, quickly buy the domain in question. Because if your niche is popular, another savvy entrepreneur may well overtake you. If your guts tell you it's a good domain name, go ahead. Nothing worse than seeing that the free domain name you liked is no longer available after a few days of thinking. Precisely because it is a complex process, avoid procrastination and when you find a domain name that you like, take it.

6. Pick a name your customers will like

A domain name should be meaningful to your audience. For example, Forever 21 is a fashion brand for women. The name Forever 21 evokes youth and freedom, the entertainment associated with this age. With this name, the brand establishes a positive emotional connection with its customers. Another example: Wish. Wish is an e-commerce platform whose name implies that you will find all the items you could want there. They sell millions of products, including a lot of gadgets that you don't even know exist. Another example with Topshop, whose name simply indicates that you are in the best place for shopping.

In general, it is important to understand your target before choosing a domain name. This involves doing market research, exchanging with your target audience, identifying your main competitors, and studying the reasons for choosing their domain name. This research can help you better understand the way of thinking of your future customers and therefore know how to establish a relationship of trust with them, thanks to a domain name that makes sense.

7. Test your ideas

Ask the opinion of those around you on your domain name. You might get some interesting feedback as well. If you are planning to expand your business internationally, check the meaning of your name in different languages. Several brands made the mistake of not doing so, which subsequently totally hampered their success in some countries. A few years ago, I was discussing with a friend an idea for a domain name that I had had for a site. She proposed a similar idea but simpler, and therefore more effective. While brainstorming your ideas and using domain name generators can be very productive, sometimes chatting with friends or family can be even more effective. If as a bonus the person you're interacting with has experience in marketing, search engine optimization, or branding, they can give you some great advice on finding an effective domain name. She might know which domain is taken or not, which will make your search easier. She will also be able to bring you ideas relevant to your brand. It's always important to get a second opinion on any domain name ideas you may have.

8. Create a name that can be a brand

When choosing your domain name, there are two strategies:

Either you find a name that designates your product while being a brand. If you search among the major e-commerce brands, you will find examples of this type, such as Bricorama or Maison du Monde. We immediately understand their sector of activity, but they are brands in their own right. Bricolage, for example, would not work because it is too generic. Beauty would also be too vague, but Beautéprivée works. And in this last example, we immediately understand that it is a beauty brand offering a premium, exclusive service. The other strategy is to choose an invented name. Your name for example, or an assumed name, like Daniel Wellington, a popular online watch store today. The downside to this strategy is that it's going to take you a lot longer to get people to understand what you're selling. So plan a significant marketing and communication budget. On the other hand, a unique name offers the advantage of exclusivity, which consumers appreciate. Plus, your brand will appear immediately when people search for it.

Important points for choosing a domain name

1. Don't limit your plans for the future

If you know from the start that your long-term goal is to build an Amazon or Cdiscount- style multistore, focus on a brand name rather than a keyword-based name. At the start, your online store will only offer products related to the chosen niche. But as you learn more about your audience, you'll start to expand your product catalog. When you think about your online business, do you imagine it will become the leader in your niche wherever it grows beyond? Do you plan: where do you see your brand in a year? In five years? Also, think of the biggest brands in the world. Do they use unique names or are they based on keywords? Microsoft, Apple, Facebook, and Google do not include keywords and yet they are among the most powerful. Do you want to create a niche brand or shop? If you go for the brand, then forget the keywords. If you want to stick to a niche, then look for the right keywords.

There is no right or wrong decision. Even if your unique name will not immediately attract traffic, it will be possible with the keywords of the content of your site anyway. You will just have to invest more in the growth in visibility of your brand, that is, in advertising.

2. Buy an unused domain name

The domain name you want to buy may be owned by someone. It's frustrating, but you can always contact the owner and buy it back. Do you want to know who owns this domain name? Use the WHOIS site to find their contact information. Those who wish to sell a domain will leave them public. If you buy a domain directly from its owner, it will probably cost you more than from a registrar. On average, count $100 for a name with an average volume of searches. The owner can accept your offer or make a counteroffer. If the search volume is high, the price it offers is worth considering. That said, it may take a little experience to spot a good investment.

3. Check the history of a domain name

Before spending your money on buying a domain, check its track record. The domain in question may have a good backlink profile, but it may also have been penalized due to the use of black hat techniques. This type of activity should be checked. There are several tools for this. I recommend Wayback Machine which allows you to see the entire history of a site and its domain. For example, you will be able to see what Twitter looked like in 2010. A very practical tool for detecting any illegal activity.

4. Check the availability of associated social media profiles

Before buying a domain, check the associated accounts on social networks. Ideally, the name of each social profile should be the same as your company name. However, it often happens that this is not possible. Harmony among all occurrences of your brand is necessary for greater credibility. Plus, your customers will find you more easily. Use tools like Namecheck to find out if your brand will find its place on various social networks. This site highlights available domain extensions and names on social platforms: Facebook, Twitter, Pinterest, Instagram, and YouTube.

5. Protect your personal information

ICANN allows users to access contact information for domain registrants. This could involve legal action or the purchase of a domain. When you register a domain name, your contact details (address and email) will be published. If you do not have an office, your home address will be made public. WHOIS has a service called WhoisGuard, which protects your data for a small annual fee. This is ideal for those who run a home business and wish to remain anonymous or those who do not want to be contacted. You will be able to join WhoisGuard through certain registrars.

6. Buy similar domain names

A lot of people ask me to share my online store. I don't and here's the reason:

A few years ago, I spent all my time building an online business. It was working well, I had stable sales. The count of our Instagram followers was exploding, everything was fine. One day someone contacted me asking for advice and I happily shared some of my experience. This person knew my online store and decided to clone it entirely, down to the name of the brand.

This scammer created several social media accounts with variations of the name. He bought followers and made this store seem more popular than mine. She copied my brand name, adding only one keyword. I blamed myself very much for sharing all this information. However, the cruel truth is that even if I hadn't done so, sooner or later copycats would have appeared. As your popularity grows, your brand's success will be noticed by people with bad intentions or people who are just looking for inspiration. Even I did. Following the failure of this first online store, I spotted another business with a very high engagement rate on social networks and I went into the same niche. It turns out to be the most popular store in all of my businesses. Nevertheless, I took care to create my brand with my name. So if you find a brand name that you love, buy all of its variations. Order the different extensions available, additional keywords, like (name) shop.com or (name) store.com. Also, think about misspelled versions of your site. Make it impossible to copy yourself.

7. Think about SEO when buying a domain name

For SEO reasons, it can be tempting to choose a domain name that relates directly to your online business or products. Nevertheless, tactics like these are tried and true and no longer work. Google's algorithm filters and penalizes webmasters who create sites with low-quality content that exactly matches the domain name. Rather than choosing terms like bestcafé.com or ticketspourdisney.com, choose a domain name that relates to your brand (you'll thank me later). If a keyword domain name can boost your traffic when you launch your site, it is a brand name that will allow you to develop over time.

The 5 best registrars for 2020

There are a lot of registrars where you can buy a free domain name in just a few clicks. Here is a list of the best registrars where you can register your free domain name... sometimes.

1. Ionos (ex 1 & 1)

Ionos is the European leader in web hosting. They offer services to create a domain name, a website, host it, and create a personalized e-mail address. Very interesting point, Ionos is the only registrar that offers a free domain name. Provided it is with an extension 'EU.' This offer is only valid for the first year. That said, the other extensions almost include a free domain name: €1 the first year and €10 per year thereafter. These prices relate to the .fr, .org extensions. and .com. They increase slightly for .shop and.co. Other advantageous features are offered, such as subdomains or simplified activation.

IONOS by 1&1

Sign in

Find your d

Check

Got a $1 and a dream?

Make it real with a .com — the world's most recognizable domain.

Get yours

WEB HOSTING
Fast. Secure. Flexible.

First month – $1
Cancel anytime

WORDPRESS
Quick to build. Easy to manage.

First month – $1
Cancel anytime

DEDICATED SERVER
Hardware meets the cloud.

First month – $200 credit
Cancel anytime

2. OVHcloud

OVH is another well-known host offering many services related to the creation of a website. OVH domain names are popular because the company offers no less than 800 extensions. A choice that will not facilitate your research! The creation and transfer of domain names start at 0.49 € per year and increase depending on the extension chosen. Again, almost a free domain name. The offer includes an email address, the Obfuscator service, which allows you to hide your personal information on WHOis and the DNSSEC security system which protects connections to your site. Finally, OVH presents different options depending on your profile: individual, professional, or reseller.

3. GoDaddy

Domain Names

Grab a .com for £0.99/1st yr.

2-year purchase required. Additional year(s) £16.14

Over 18 million users trust GoDaddy to manage their websites. A number that motivates them to subscribe to their many services, ranging from domain registration to security and marketing. Chances are, you won't be signing up for domains alone. The first prices start at €1 to reserve a free domain name for the first year. But then watch your bills, because the costs can quickly increase.

4. NameCheap

NameCheap provides domain name registration, hosting, management, and other services for more than 5 million domain names worldwide. This very ergonomic site offers a very pleasant user experience and will allow you to find your domain in a few clicks, starting at $ 0.88. Please note, the site is in English. Another advantage is, if the domain name that interests you is taken, you can try to buy it directly through NameCheap. You grant all their services by visiting the site.

5. Shopify

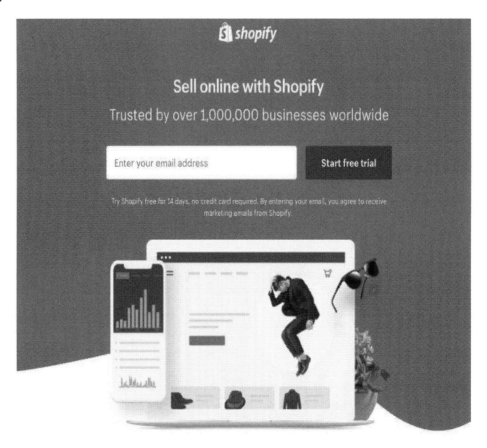

If you are developing an online store, then you will be able to register your domain name through Shopify. If you don't have any idea of domain names, you will surely find some using our free domain name generator. To buy your domain name on Shopify, you first enter the name that interests you in the generator. You can also add keywords. A list of names will then appear. While not all of the names will necessarily include your keywords, they will be relevant to your niche anyway. Once you've chosen your name, reserve it on Shopify. You will then need to enter your e-mail, password, and the name of the online store. You will then have to enter your bank and postal details to receive the fruits of your first sales. And There you go! You have just purchased your first domain name. You can start working on your online store right away.

Chapter Three

Installing WordPress and Account Setup through Control Panel

WordPress is a quick and easy tool for creating blogs, websites, e-commerce. Fast and intuitive, it is the most powerful and the most widespread CMS. What is that supposed to mean? Content management system, that is software for creating websites that do not require any programming knowledge.

WordPress is used by web agencies around the world. Despite this, creating a site with WordPress is easy. In this guide, I will give you the basic suggestions: if you want to dig deeper into some aspects, you can always contact me! Before we dive into optimizations, it's important to understand that not all WordPress sites are the same. This is why a lot of users have problems because you cannot approach every problem in the same way. We always give WordPress sites a classification: static or dynamic. Let's take a look at the differences between these two types of sites first.

Most sites are static

Static sites generally include sites such as blogs, small business sites, low volume news sites, personal sites, photography sites, etc. By static, we mean that the data on these WordPress sites don't change very often (maybe a few times a day). Even a good portion of our Kinsta site would be considered a static site.

This becomes all the more important as many requests can be served directly from the server cache at lightning speed! Don't worry, we'll cover the topic of caching later in the following. This means that they will have fewer database calls and not as many resources will be needed to achieve google performance.

Very dynamic sites

On the other hand, we have very dynamic sites. These include eCommerce stores (WooCommerce or Easy Digital Downloads), community sites, membership sites, forums (bbPress or BuddyPress), and learning management systems (LMS). By dynamic, we mean that the data on these WordPress sites changes frequently (server exchanges take place every few minutes or even every second). This means that all requests made to the server cannot be served directly from the cache and require additional server resources and database requests.

These sites also typically have a large number of concurrent visitors and sessions. On an information or business WordPress site that is mostly static, a visitor can stay five or ten minutes until they find what they need (and that's a high number, usually bounce rates are much higher). On dynamic sites, the opposite is true. Visitors usually come to the site to engage with something or someone. If they're taking an online course, it's not uncommon for them to stay there for hours. You can see where this is taking us. Visitors connected simultaneously to your WordPress hosting add up quickly. To make matters worse, then you have a large number of concurrent visitors in addition to a "non-cacheable content" problem.

A Step-by-step Guide on how to Install WordPress and Continue with Building of your Website

Once you've established the content for your site, and purchased the domain and hosting, you can start building a site with WordPress! At this point, you need to install WordPress. Installing WordPress is a straightforward procedure, but should be done step by step:

- Download WordPress in on the official site;
- Create a database. To do this, go to your hosting control panel, select the appropriate item (depending on the hosting provider you contacted) and assign a name and password to your database;

- Open the WordPress archive you downloaded: it's a zip file, unzip it. Open the folder: find the wp-config-sample.php file and rename it to wp-config.php;
- Open the wp-config.php file with a text editor (Windows Notepad is great too) and make these changes: In the string define ('DB_NAME', 'database_name_name_here'); instead of database_name_here enter the name of your WordPress hosting database; In the string define ('DB_USER', 'username_here'); instead of username_here enter the username of the WordPress database administrator; in the string define ('DB_PASSWORD', 'password_here'); In the string define ('DB_HOST', 'localhost'); overrides the corresponding value (for many hosts, like Aruba, it's always localhost, but there are exceptions); Under the section "Unique Authentication and Salting Keys ", enter the security keys as shown on the WordPress site.
- In the string define ('DB_NAME', 'database_name_name_here'); instead of database_name_here enter the name of your WordPress hosting database;
- In the string define ('DB_USER', 'username_here'); instead of username_here enter the username of the administrator of the WordPress database;
- In the string define ('DB_PASSWORD', 'password_here'); instead of password_here enter the password of your WordPress database;
- In the string define ('DB_HOST', 'localhost'); replace the corresponding value (for most hosts, like Aruba, it's always localhost, but there are exceptions);
- Under the "Unique Authentication and Salting Keys" section, enter the security keys as shown on the WordPress site.
- In the control panel of your WordPress hosting, select the file manager (or the Download tool) and upload the files contained in the WordPress folder in the main directory of the site;
- Once the operation is complete, connect to the following address: intuition address/wp-admin/install.php (eg www.marcoloprete. it/wp-admin/install.php). This will launch the WordPress installation. During the procedure, you will need to enter the site title (you can always change it), the username and password to access the WordPress control panel, and your email address

FIRST STEPS: INDEXING

To access the WordPress control panel, type in your browser's address bar:

address/admin-wp-address[s

Enter your username and password here, and voila: welcome to the administrative area of your site!

The control panel of your new site!

Before creating articles and pages, a tip: work incognito! With an option, you can "hide" the site from search engines and block indexing. How are you doing that? From the control panel, go to Settings > Read, scroll down and check "Discourage search engines from indexing this site". (I did this myself before uploading this article: if someone had Google "Marco Loprete" they wouldn't have found any results related to this blog.)

Check the box and Google won't see you!

When the articles, pages, and content are ready, and therefore you are ready to launch your website, do not forget to remove the checkmark: this way you will have the possibility of appearing in Google results and from other search engines. Before you create a site with WordPress, make sure you can work undisturbed!

PERMANENT LINK

Another very useful change that I recommend you make immediately is the permalink. It is a question of deciding what form will take the URL (addresses) of your site. WordPress, by default, adopts this structure: http://nomesito/ ?P=123malink.php.

You will agree that from this URL it is quite difficult to understand what the page is about: much clearer. It is, therefore, better to adopt what is called "speaking addresses". What is that? Still, in the WordPress control panel, go to Settings; Permalink and select "Item name" (or, if you have special needs, "Custom structure"). This way you will also have clear and captivating screams!

Installing a New Theme and Plugins On WordPress

There are several ways to install a WordPress template but today we are going to settle for the simplest method that will suit everyone. I will nevertheless distinguish two cases: the installation of a free WordPress theme from the WordPress.org site directory and the installation of a paid template for WordPress. To install a free theme, it's very simple, follow these steps to download, install, and activate your graphic theme for your WordPress site:

1. Go to the administration of your site in WordPress then click in the left menu on Appearance then on Themes. Click on the Add button.

2. Choose the theme you want to install through the theme search engine. Then hover over the chosen theme and click on the Install button, which will appear on hover.

3. Wait for the installation time, which may vary depending on your hosting and your internet connection. Once done, you just have to press the Activate button to replace your old theme with your brand new WordPress template.

There you have it: your new theme has been uploaded to your site's hosting then installed and activated. You now have a brand new graphic design for your WordPress website!

Install a paid WordPress theme (Pro/Premium version)

The situation is slightly different for installing a paid theme, whether it is called Pro or Premium. You can also use the WordPress theme installation procedure below to install a free template downloaded beforehand. If you purchased a WordPress template, you should have received it as a zip archive. Warning! First, open your zip archive to see what it contains. There is a good chance that your archive contains several files (license, PSD, documentation etc...). The folder that interests us is generally called theme (original!). This folder will itself contain a zip file. This file will have to be sent to your WordPress site.

Here's how to install your paid WordPress theme:

1. Go to the back-office of your site then click in the left menu on Appearance then on Themes. Click on the Add button.

2. Then click on the Upload a topic button.

3. In the open interface click on the Browse button then select the previously identified zip file from your computer.

4. Click on the Install button once the file has uploaded to your site and is no longer grayed out.

5. Your theme will now appear in the list of themes installed on your website, you just have to click on the Activate button to use your new paid WordPress theme.

Note that it is also quite possible to install a WordPress theme using an FTP client like Filezilla. But this procedure is a bit more complicated for newbies, I will probably cover it in a future article. If you want to dig deeper into the subject, search your favorite search engine and you will easily find information on the web. If everything went well (and this is generally the case with WordPress which handles the installation of themes very well), your WordPress theme is now installed, well done.

Configure your WordPress theme

You can (and should!) Now configure your WordPress theme to customize your WP theme. Some themes have a dedicated entry in the Appearance menu of the administration with adjustable parameters. In any case, to have access to the options of your theme, go to Appearance then Customize.

Here, you can configure different options of your WordPress theme including:

- Site identity
- General theme settings
- Header/ logo/favicon images

- Set the homepage of your WordPress site (display of a static page or the latest articles)
- Adjustment of colors, background colors, fonts according to the options offered by your WP theme
- Widgets

Step-by-Step Guide in Installing Plug-ins

Before installing WordPress plugins, it is good to remember what a plugin is. A WordPress plugin, which is called an extension, is a specific feature that you will add to your WordPress. Once you have installed your WordPress you immediately have a ready-to-use site with basic functions. You are therefore going to install additional plugins to fully customize your CMS, with a contact form, for example, an image gallery, Widgets, administrative functions, etc.

Where to find WordPress plugins (extensions)?

There are tens of thousands of free or paid (premium) WordPress plugins. Before embarking on a search that could take hours and end up disappointing you, ask yourself the question: "I want to add what function and for what?" .Check that this function does not already exist by default in WordPress or the theme that you have activated. I have already seen dozens of unnecessary extensions on certain sites, which weighs down the system and therefore your performance.

The official directory of WordPress plugins

This directory contains, to date, more than 48,000 free WordPress plugins. In other words, you have the choice and you will surely find the extension you are looking for.

Since the official language of WordPress is English, you need to do keyword research in its language to get relevant results.

Websites to buy WordPress plugins

If you cannot find what you are looking for with WordPress, other websites offer WordPress plugins for purchase, either on platforms or directly on sites dedicated to a plugin.

Here is a non-exhaustive list:

- Codecanyon: https://codecanyon.net/tags/plugin?category=wordpress&referrer=search &utf8=%E2%9C%93&view=list
- WooCommerce: https://woocommerce.com/plugins/
- Graph Paper Press: https://graphpaperpress.com/extensions/sell-media/
- ithemes: https://ithemes.com/find/plugins/
- Wp-rocket: https://wp-rocket.me/
- Wp-types: https://wp-types.com/

- Wcpos: http://wcpos.com/

Tip: Use your favorite search engine to start your search by typing "XX WordPress plugin" (Replace XX with the keyword (s) of the desired function. Ex: slider WordPress plugin).

Install a free plugin from the WordPress directory

- In the administration (the BackOffice) of your WordPress you find the official WordPress directory by going to "Extensions> Add".

- In the "extensions search engine" enter the name of the plugin or the keywords in English of the desired theme. In this example, we are going to add additional features to the WordPress text editor with the "TinyMCE Advanced" plugin.

- Locate the WordPress plugin you want to install and click the Install button. Once installed, do not forget to activate the extension by clicking the Activate button.

- Your WordPress plugin is now installed and activated. Some plugins need to be configured, we will see this part later.

If you want to test plugins before installing them on your live site, I advise you to create a site locally on your computer, so you can compare extensions and get an idea of their functionality without risk for your online site.

Common Bugs You May experience after installing your website

PHP errors and database errors can manifest as a white screen, a blank screen with no information, commonly known in the WordPress community as the WordPress White Screen of Death (WSOD). This is the most impressive bug because, without a clear error message, panic can quickly take over. Before resorting to desperate measures, there are 2 probable reasons for this problem:

A plugin causes compatibility issues. If you can access admin, try disabling all your plugins and then re-enabling them one by one. If you no longer have access to the administration panel, connect to your website using FTP. Locate the wp-content/plugins folder and rename the "Plugins" folder to "plugins_old". This will deactivate all your Plugins.

Your WordPress theme may be the source of the problem. This is especially likely if you experience the White Screen of Death after activating a new theme. Log in to the WordPress administration and activate the default WordPress theme. If you can't access administration, access your website via FTP and navigate to the / wp-content / themes/folder. Rename the active theme folder, this will deactivate it. If you do not know what you are doing, seek professional help.

Error while connecting to the database

The error making a connection to the database is usually caused by an error in your wp-config.php file. Access your site in your FTP client. Open wp-config.php and make sure the following information is correct:

- Name of the database
- Database username
- Database password
- Database host

If you are sure your configuration is correct, and you know what you are doing, you can try resetting your MySQL password manually.

- **The site is not referenced**

Google, Bing, and other search engines don't know about your site. It is however vital! There are three main reasons why your site is a ghost on the search engines. Fortunately, not all of these reasons are equally serious and some can be easily resolved. Here is what can prevent your site from showing up in search results:

1. Your site is not yet indexed (too recent)

It can take up to four weeks for it to start showing up in search engine results. Are you impatient? You can create an account on webmaster tools. When you register and enter your sitemap.xml URL, you can request to browse your site. However, there are so many requests that the feature does not always work immediately.

2. Your website has "no index" tags

Ah, the dumpling! You can indeed use a code to tell search engines not to index your site (or specific pages). If you or the person who designed your site added this code - for example to not index the site under construction - that would explain why it does not appear in search results. They must be removed!

3. Your website has been penalized and removed from Google.

Google may temporarily or permanently remove sites from its index and search results if it believes it is required to do so by law, if the sites do not meet Google's quality guidelines or for other reasons, such as if sites interfere with the ability of users to find relevant information. Here are the different ways Google can remove your site from search results :

- **Deindexed:** When your domain is completely removed from Google.
- **Penalized:** When your domain or page still exists but none of your pages can be found by direct search queries. This penalty can be automatic using the Google algorithm or applied manually by a Google quality engineer.
- **Sandboxed:** Your domain or page has not been deindexed or penalized, but the traffic you are receiving from Google suddenly drops dramatically.

If your site is blocked because it violates Google guidelines, it can notify you using Search Console in Webmaster Tools. If you receive a message telling you that your site is violating its quality guidelines, you can edit your site to meet those guidelines, and then submit your site for reconsideration. If you are unsure how to go about it, it is once again strongly advised that you call in a WordPress expert.

- The site is blocked for maintenance

A common bug: You update your site and extensions, and those updates seem to be over. You go to your site and pattern! Here it is stuck in maintenance mode, and nothing in the admin allows you to get out of it. Fortunately, it is quite easy to get out of this bad situation: Go and check the FTP site, in the root directory of your site, if there is not yet a .maintenance file. If so, deleting that file should resolve the issue.

- **The site is very slow**

So there, you might as well warn you, there are dozens of reasons for this. The best will probably be to request an audit from a professional so that the diagnosis is known. However, there are a few things you can check without requiring advanced knowledge.

1. Install a cache system

WordPress pages are dynamic. This means that they are built on the fly every time someone visits an article or page on your website. To build your pages, WordPress must go through a process to find the required information, put it together, and then display it to your user. This process involves a lot of steps, and it can slow down your website, especially when you have multiple people visiting it at the same time. That is why it is recommended to use a caching plugin. Caching can make your WordPress site 2x to 5x faster. There are several and all of them are effective!

2. Optimize images

Images bring your content to life and help drive engagement. However, if your images aren't optimized, they could be doing you more harm than good. Unoptimized images are one of the most common speed issues you encounter on newbie websites. Before uploading a photo directly from your camera, use photo editing software to optimize your images on the web. In their original format, these photos can carry enormous weight. It is possible to compress them without losing quality and reduce their weight quite dramatically!

3. Make your updates

It is important to keep your plugins, and WordPress, up to date: some updates indeed include notable improvements in the loading speed of different scripts.

4. Use excerpts instead of the whole text

By default, WordPress displays the full content of each post on your home page and archives. This means that your homepage, categories, tags, and other archive pages will load more slowly. Another disadvantage of showing full articles on these pages is that users do not feel the need to visit the "real" article. This can reduce the number of pages viewed and the time your users spend on your site. To speed up page load time, you can configure your site to display snippets instead of the full content.

- **The site is constantly spammed**

If you allow comments on your site, you may receive spam. As your site grows in popularity, spam is even likely to become an even bigger problem. There are many types of comment spam, but most of it is automated, posted by spambots that use short, generic messages to include links. No matter what form it takes, comment spam is a real problem because:

- When your comment sections are filled with spam, it makes it harder for legitimate visitors to have conversations.
- Leaving spam comments on your content makes your site unprofessional.
- Many of these comments contain malicious links, designed to trick visitors into providing personal information.

You must do everything in your power to prevent comment spam from appearing on your WordPress site. Fortunately, it is not difficult, once you know the right techniques. You will be able to do a lot in the "Settings" -> "Discussion" section of your administration panel.

1. Reduce the number of links allowed per message

Most comment spam is designed to add links to your comments section and get people to click on them. Therefore, one way to combat spam is to allow fewer links in your comments. Legitimate visitors will also be prevented from viewing many links, but slowing down spammers may be worth this potential inconvenience. From the administration, you can adjust this parameter. A link is already good, right? This spam can also harm your SEO, so don't hesitate to add UGC link attributes.

2. Create a list of "blacklisted" words

Spam comments contain a lot of recognizable keywords. It's easy to spot them and prevent them from showing up on your website. You can simply create a blacklist of words, and your site will mark any comments containing any of them as spam. Of course, it is important to choose the words on your blacklist carefully, so as not to erase legitimate comments.

3. Restrict commenting privileges to registered users

The goal of most spammers is to post on as many pages and sites as possible. If you can make it harder to add their comments to your site, they'll move on to the next target. You can limit the privilege of commenting to people who have registered on your site. This places an additional barrier between spammers and your comments section. Captcha is also a good way to limit spammers, there are also several alternatives to Captcha.

4. Set up a comment moderation system

Comment moderation is when some (or all) comments need to be approved by someone before they are allowed to appear on your site. If you have the time and resources, it can pay off.

5. Use an anti-spam plugin

Finally, I would be remiss if I did not mention spam plugins. These tools can be a powerful way to stop comment spam and can take care of sorting the good comments from the bad ones for you. Many WordPress installations come with Akismet and for good reason!

6. Change to another comment system

This method won't work for all sites, but some third-party commenting systems, like Disqus, can help eliminate most spam for you. Another option is to use Facebook comments on your site.

These problems, while common, do not all have the same severity, nor the same repercussions on your site. While some are easily bypassed, others require advanced knowledge of WordPress: you can ask a freelancer to do a one-off assignment for you.

WooCommerce Plug-in

WordPress is historically designed for the creation of content, that is to say, the edition of sites like blogs or magazines. WordPress is not called WordPress for anything. It is however possible to create an e-commerce site using WordPress, thanks to the multiple extensions (= plugins) which have gradually been offered by developers. Moreover, this incredible wealth of plugins can be explained by the fact that WordPress is open-source software. Unlike what we observe with publishers like Shopify or Wix who are "proprietary" editors, anyone can offer a new theme or plugin designed for WordPress. You can also modify all the core elements of your WordPress site. In short, this is an extremely flexible and modular editor that meets all needs and allows you to do whatever you want. You will find dozens, and even hundreds, of e-commerce plugins designed for WordPress: WP eCommerce, Cart 66, Jigoshop, MarketPress, Shopp, WP shop, etc. As everyone can offer their plugin, there is of course anything and everything on WordPress plugin platforms. In this case, the few examples of e-commerce plugins that we just mentioned are all good e-commerce plugins. They have a lot of quality, some flaws, but all do pretty well.

However, there is an e-commerce plugin that stands out. This plugin is WooCommerce, launched in 2011 and published by WooThemes (acquired by Automaticin 2015, the creator of WordPress). It is, in our opinion (but not only in our opinion!), The most powerful, most flexible, and most complete e-commerce plugin. We can do almost anything with this extension, as we will have the opportunity to see. Powerful, WooCommerce is also very popular (which is revealing in itself about the quality of the plugin). It is even, by far, the most popular e-commerce plugin. Today, nearly 30% of e-commerce sites in the world are powered by WooCommerce. This represents, still worldwide, more than

700,000 sites (and more than 13 million downloads according to the publisher of the plugin).

Before starting the tutorial, remember that WooCommerce is free, although some extensions of WooCommerce require payment. If you need complex and specific features (for example an advanced inventory manager), you will probably have to go through the purchase of extensions. Remember also that creating a WooCommerce site is different from creating an e-commerce site from a platform specifically dedicated to e-commerce (such as Wix, Shopify, Prestashop, Magento, etc.). WooCommerce is especially recommended if you want to:

Have complete control over your website. With proprietary software, you are often limited. For example, you cannot always adjust SEO parameters (meta description tag, URL, etc.). And then, more generally, you are very limited in modifying the code (example: adding tags in the header, etc.). WooCommerce is WordPress, so you can edit everything, customize everything, manage every-thing.

To be able to have an e-commerce site which is not only an e-commerce site but a site that also hosts a blog, various and varied pages, etc. By using WordPress, you benefit from the best blog editor around the world!

Do not pay commissions on your sales or a monthly subscription, as is the case with all proprietary software.

Being able to start small and build your site as your business grows. WooCommerce makes it possible to create very simple sites, but can also meet all the complex needs possible and imaginable. Regarding payment management, for example, you can start with very easy-to-manage tools like PayPal, Amazon Payments, or Google Wallet before implementing SSL technology after a certain level of development.

Install and configure the Woocommerce plugin on your WordPress site

Downloading and installing WooCommerce on your WordPress site is extremely easy. You just have to go to your WordPress interface (your dashboard), and go to the "Extensions" tab ==> "Add". You type WooCommerce into the search bar. The plugin appears right away. Click "Install Now" and activate it. Once the WooCommerce plugin is activated, you can launch the WooCommerce wizard, which will allow you to make the first settings. A WooCommerce site needs several structuring pages, such as the store page, the cart page, the order page, or the "my account" page.

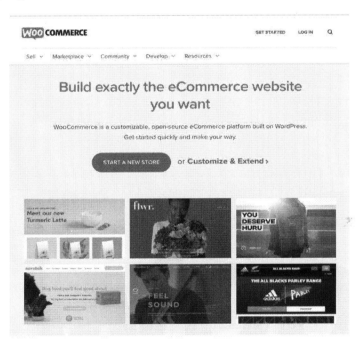

WooCommerce offers you at the start of the wizard to automatically generate these pages. Accept by clicking on "Continue". You can customize these pages later.

- You must then specify the location of your store, the currency used, and the units of measure for the weight and dimensions:
- You must then indicate whether you offer a delivery service (which it probably is) and whether you charge VAT.

Last step: payment. Setting up payments is perhaps the most delicate step when creating an e-commerce site. We recommend that you add PayPal to get started. You can then add other payment methods. That is, for the basic configurations. Needless to say, the job is not done. A WooCommerce site is mostly made up of product pages. To familiarize yourself immediately with the product page editor, click on "Create your first product!"

If you are already a WordPress user, the product page editor should not take you away from it all. It is, more or less (the important thing is in this nuance, as we will see), the same editor that is used to create blog posts. We will come back to this editor later. But first, let's focus on some aspects of settings. You may see a block displayed explaining that your theme is not compatible with WooCommerce (red box).

If this message appears, you must change the theme. Otherwise, your pages may display badly and some features may bug. We come back to this point in the next paragraph. Install the Google Analytics by MonsterInsights plugin and the Yoast SEO plugin now if you haven't already. The first will allow you to link the data of your WooCommerce site to Google Analytics, one of the most powerful web analysis tools (completely free). Thanks to Google Analytics, you will be able to know more about your visitors, their behavior, their level of engagement, etc. Google Analytics allows for many other things. A little advice, If you want to go a step further in web analysis and be able to use specifically e-commerce monitoring indicators, install WooCommerce Google Analytics Integration instead. This plugin allows you to track your orders directly in Google Analytics.

Creating the structure of your WooCommerce online store

On WooCommerce, you can configure the structure of your permanent URLs ("permalinks") in a completely personalized way. This helps to give a clear and coherent structure to your store. This is a real plus, especially for SEO. This is much more efficient than unstructured URLs which consist of agglutination of incomprehensible numbers, letters, and signs. To configure the permanent URLs for your product pages, you need to go to WooCommerce ==> Settings ==> Products ==> Display. You should do this procedure from the start, because it is difficult, once you have already created several pages, to change the structure of your URLs:

WooCommerce needs a page that lists and displays all of your products and categories. A page is created by default by WooCommerce. This is the "Shop" page. You can rename this page if you want by going to Pages ==> All Pages. In any case, this page is not intended to be seen by your visitors. Unless you want to make it your homepage, that's not necessarily a great idea. Either way, this "Shop" page (or call it whatever you want) must exist. You need to configure it. To do this, click on "product permalink" (red box):

You land on a page where you can configure your product permalinks:

The structure of product permalinks is different from the structure of WordPress post permalinks. For example, if you have a blog section on your WooCommerce site with a "shoes" category, the permalink structure will be as follows:

your-site-woocommerce.com/categories/shoes

If at the same time you have a "shoes" category on the store part of your WooCommerce site, the permanent URL will look like this:

your-site-woocommerce.com/category-product/shoes

Now that you have checked and possibly customized the structure of your product permalinks, let's move on to the next step:

Choose a WordPress theme compatible with WooCommerce

WooCommerce is a WordPress plugin, we have seen it. A plugin is an extension (a kind of small software) that allows you to add new functionality to WordPress. The theme is the element that controls the design of your site, that is to say, the way your site appears to your visitors. WooCommerce adds loads of functionality to WordPress, but the concern is that some themes are not built to incorporate these features. You must therefore absolutely choose a theme that is compatible with WooCommerce. Otherwise, all the work you have done on the interface (the back office) will have been for nothing. You will notice at one point or another (quite quickly in fact) that your site is showing badly and will have to start from zero with a new theme.

A little advice, you must choose a WooCommerce compatible theme from the start of creating your WooCommerce site. In case of hesitation, do not slow down the project, choose StoreFront the theme made by the publisher of WooCommerce. A theme that is not only compatible with WooCommerce but also sufficiently versatile and customizable. To choose your theme, you have several possibilities:

Buy a theme offered by WooThemes, the historic publisher of WooCommerce. All WooThemes themes are paid, but high quality. Except one: Storefront, which we highly recommend.

Search for a theme directly from your WordPress back office, by going to Appearance ==> Themes ==> Add a theme. You can choose a default and free WordPress theme like Twenty-Twelve. This is the most economical solution, but it requires some technical knowledge (you will have to adapt the theme for WooCommerce).

Buy a theme in a marketplace. We recommend the ThemeForest platform, which has the merit of offering themes specifically designed for WooCommerce. More generally, ThemeForest is one of the best theme stores. Also, discover our selection of 30 WordPress themes to create an e-commerce site. All of them are compatible with WooCommerce.

Configure your WooCommerce store settings

The configuration of the parameters of your WooCommerce site is done directly from your WordPress dashboard, by going to WooCommerce ==> Settings. You will notice that there are a lot of default settings. These include the settings you configured in the software wizard, but also settings automatically installed by WooCommerce. Start by going through the sections and sub-sections of all the tabs on the "Settings" page to check the default settings and possibly change them. You can also customize the design of your store (the shape of the buttons for example) by modifying the CSS (the style.css file). It requires technical knowledge. We also recommend that you check the box "Activate the lightbox for product images" in the "Products" tab of the settings menu. This feature allows Internet users to click on the images of your products to enlarge them without leaving your site.

Product pages are, again, the most important parts of your e-commerce site. You need to spend some time adjusting these pages, in the "Products" tab. Pay particular attention to the configuration of the dimensions of the images (in the "Display" sub-tab). You must verify that the images of your products display correctly on your site, on product pages, on catalog pages, etc. Spend time on this point before importing the hundreds or thousands of images in your catalog. WooCommerce offers very comprehensive documentation on the subject. There is no question of going into the details of all the configuration elements here. Most are self-explanatory and should be customized to suit your needs and tastes. Do not hesitate, if you block on a particular element, to refer to the excellent documentation offered by WooCommerce, accessible at this address. Take into account all the details to get the most out of the features and options that WooCommerce gives you.

The configuration of automatic emails sent to your customers

The settings of your WooCommerce site are not only made from the "Settings" section of the WooCommerce tab. You should also take into account the sections "System status" and "Extensions". The "System Status" section allows you to access technical information about your WooCommerce site and check its configuration status. To learn more, we recommend reading this article. The "Extensions" section is what makes WooCommerce great software. WooCommerce offers a gigantic store of extensions (= plugins) that allow you to add new e-commerce features.

The richness of this extension store allows you to avoid having to contact a developer each time you want to add an element to your site (a new payment method for example). Some extensions are free, others pay. But do you say that the price of the extension that interests you will always be less salty than the invoice of a developer! We invite you now to browse the extensions store to identify extensions that may be of interest to you. The extensions are classified by category. Now that you have completed the settings and installed your extensions (which takes time), you will need to create your product pages.

Creating the product pages for your WooCommerce site

The design of your product pages depends a lot on the theme used. It is in the menu Items ==> Add that you must go to edit your different product pages. WooCommerce allows you to create very comprehensive product pages, including all the necessary details about your products and their attributes. As we said previously, the editor is identical to the one used for classic WordPress sites (non-e-commerce).

You must, for each product page, define the title, write a description of the product, choose the category and tags (labels) to which the product is attached, add product images, etc. You can customize the URL path. Until then, editing a product page is done the same way as editing a blog post on WordPress. What changes is the "Product Data" block, which appears under the central part of the editor? This is also, what makes one of the great strengths of WooCommerce. This block is used to manage the entire elements specific to the product pages: price, delivery, stock status, dimensions and weight, options (color, size, etc.), complementary/similar products, etc. This block allows you to create very complete product pages giving all the information your customers need. We invite you to take a look at all the tabs in this block to familiarize yourself with and optimize your product pages.

You will find that creating a product page on WooCommerce is a snap. It will not take you long to get to grips with this editor. If you want to offer multiple products on your WooCommerce site (which it probably is!), you will need to organize these products into different categories. To do this, you must go to Products ==> Categories. What is very convenient, especially if you have a large catalog, is that you have the option of creating sub-categories.

I want to emphasize in this guide the key points taken into account when creating a WooCommerce site: the first settings, the choice of the theme, the peculiarities of the product page editor, etc. We could have spent more time on certain technical points, such as setting the delivery options for example. But that would have unnecessarily lengthened this guide. To go further, we advise you to refer once again to the excellent documentation made available to you by WooCommerce.

Chapter Four

Setting Up WooCommerce Payment Methods

In this chapter, we will discuss a step-by-step guide in setting up Payment Method using WooCommerce in the United States Using PayPal Payment Method. Among its many native features, WooCommerce allows you to accept payments with PayPal. You can activate this option in WooCommerce Settings, via the Payments tab. On the other hand, be careful: WooCommerce specifies that you will need a PayPal Professional account (Business Account) for the service to work.

So far, you have surely opted for a Personal account. To operate the switch, go to the Account tab of your PayPal account (accessible from the cogwheel, at the top right of the page). Then click on Opt for a Professional account. You can then open a dedicated Pro account with a new email address, or upgrade your account while keeping the same email. After this professional work, remember to configure the PayPal option on your WordPress administration. The most important thing is to enter the email address linked to your PayPal Pro account.

Once everything is good for you, you will find that the PayPal Standard payment method will redirect your customers to PayPal to proceed to pay for their order. As a result, your visitors will leave your site, which is not great for your conversions (a specific action that you want your visitors to perform, such as a purchase for example). By multiplying the steps to accomplish before payment, you risk losing some along the way. Suddenly, your turnover may reduce a little.

To solve this problem, you can use an extension. To simplify the order flow and prevent your visitors from going to Paypal.com to pay for their purchases, you can use a dedicated plugin. The problem is, there are dozens of them. Frankly, to be polite, this is a mess. PayPal Advanced, PayPal Checkout, PayPal Pro, PayPal Here: there is PayPal everywhere and we do not understand much. Also, each extension has its specificities. For example, some will only work for companies located in the United States. Fortunately, to make things easier for you, WooCommerce has had a good idea to put together a small summary table with some in-house extensions. Among them, we note the presence of PayPal Checkout, which you will find on the official directory under this name: "WooCommerce PayPal Checkout Payment Gateway."

WooCommerce PayPal Checkout Payment Gateway
Par WooCommerce

Free and developed by the WooCommerce team, it is active on more than 800,000 sites and allows you to keep your visitors on your page when ordering.

Its mode of operation is simple: a modal window (which opens in the highlighting of the page) will be displayed as soon as your visitors begin the payment procedure, whether in your cart or on the description page of your product. Thanks to this, they will be able to pay for their purchases without going elsewhere. On your side, you will increase your chances of maximizing your conversions.

This section explains the installation, configuration, and use of the WooCommerce PayPal payment module.

Before starting the installation, make sure you have all the following necessary data:

- A Sandbox account for your testing (see below)
- A productive PayPal account
- WooCommerce payment module
- Access data to your server and store

It is important to follow the following steps strictly to ensure use in compliance with safety regulations.

The installation consists of the following steps:

1. Setting up a PayPal Sandbox account for your tests

2. Configuring the basic parameters of the payment module

3. Configuring payment methods

4. A test purchase

5. If the test was successful, you can insert the details of the productive account.

Setting up a sandbox account with PayPal and creating users

Before you start the installation, you must set up a Sandbox account. With this account, you will be able to test the module. If you want to start immediately with the integration of the live account, you can skip this passage.

1. Create an account in developer.paypal.com

2. Log in with your new PayPal account. You can now create a

Sandbox account under Sandbox > Accounts

3. We recommend setting up a business and personal Sandbox account

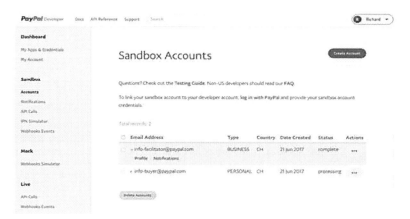

API credential Section in Setting up PayPal Payment Account (Sandbox Account) to receive Payments

For you to use all the features offered, you need to configure a user API. This is done automatically by PayPal. You can find the merchant account details under Sandbox > Accounts >Profile (below the email address). A new window, as in the image below will open. Copy the displayed data from the API Credentials tab to a separate file.

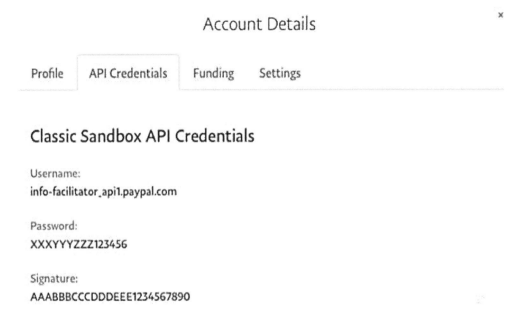

PayPal Account setup

To configure the WooCommerce main module you need your PayPal email Address, API Username, API Password, and API passphrase.

API Access Live PayPal account

You can find all the data mentioned above in Preferences > Account Settings > my sales > API Access > Update > show API signature. Please note that this will only be visible if you have a professional PayPal account. Copy the data to a separate file or use them directly for the main module configuration.

View or Remove API Signature   Back to My Profile

 Developers: Do not share your credential information with anyone. Store in a secure location with limited access.

For preconfigured shopping carts: Copy and paste the API username, password, and signature into your shopping cart configuration or administration screen.

For building custom shopping carts: Store the following credential information in a secure location with limited access.

Credential	API Signature
API Username	Show
API Password	Show
Signature	Show
Request Date	20. Aug 2012 10:49:33 GMT+02:00

[Done] [Remove]

Setting up Payment Gateway for Ecommerce Websites in India

Collecting payments online has become much easier with the multiple payment solutions available on the market, and more and more emerging. To make it easier for their online shoppers, it is now important for startups to have more ways to collect their payments online.

A good payment solution for your startup will be one that charges low transaction fees and offers a seamless payment experience. A solution that can offer them a free setup (no monthly fees), which does not limit them to the volume of transactions on the website - low or high. The best payment gateway for e-commerce websites in India will be the one that gives you more than a traditional payment gateway:

- Instant and paperless account setup,
- Quick resolution center to settle disputes between buyers,
- More Happy Startups using their solution.

That's why I recommend Instamojo as the best payment solution for startups.

How to Install Instamojo Plugin on WordPress

This section describes how to install the plugin and make it work. Make sure that you have installed the WooCommerce plugin and that it is activated. Without WooCommerce, this plugin will not work. Search for "Instamojo Payment Gateway for WooCommerce" in the WordPress Plugin directory or download it.

Install the plugin.

Activate the plugin via the WordPress 'Plugins' menu.

Once the plugin is installed and activated, you will be able to access a new menu in the configuration called "Instamojo Payment Gateway for WooCommerce."

Settings

- Now go to the Settings tab of WooCommerce (left sidebar on your WordPress dashboard) -> Settings -> Payment -> Instamojo.
- Enable/Disable - Check this box to enable this plugin.
- Title: The name of the add-on that the buyer sees during checkout.
- Description - Additional description related to this payment method, for example: "Pay with CC / DB / NB and wallets".
- Client ID and Client Secret - Client Secret and Client ID can be generated on the Integrations page.
- Test mode: if enabled, you can use our sandbox environment to test payments. Note that in this case, you need to use Client Secret and Client ID of the test account, not production.

How to get API Credentials Information from Instamojo to setup Payments Method with WooCommerce

The first step is to Login to your Instamojo account. Secondly, click on the API & plugins then click on Generate credentials >>>Choose a platform (in this case, WooCommerce/Wordpress).

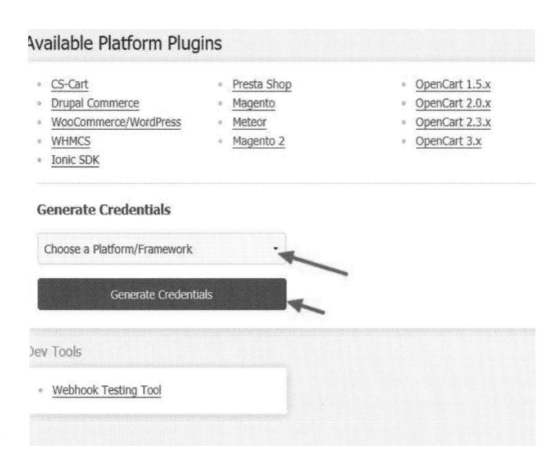

You will receive a private Auth token coupled with an API key. Ensure you copy these details.

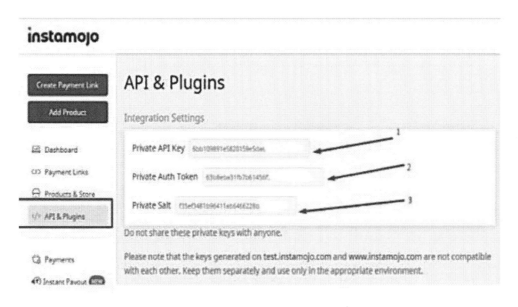

Paste the copied detail on the Multiple Payment Solutions for your WooCommerce Plugin.

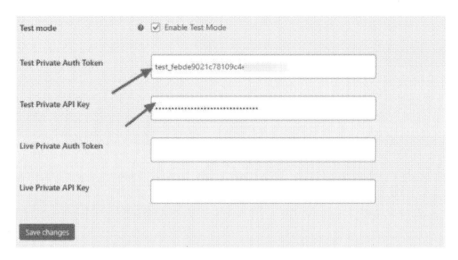

Setting up Pages and adding them as Menu Items

An online store requires different specific pages from the beginning to the end of the online order. We are therefore going to create these. In the "Pages" module of WordPress, create the following pages one by one, adding nothing other than the title inside them:

- Store: the home page of your online store
- Cart: the page containing the shopping cart with the items added by the customer
- Order: the page in which your customer will add their delivery and online payment information
- My account: (optional) a kind of profile page for customers who want to create an account on your site to facilitate their future orders
- General conditions of sale and use: the page containing the general conditions of sale and use of your site.

When these pages are created, you must associate them in the configuration of WooCommerce. To associate the "Shop" page, open WooCommerce -> Settings -> Products. To link the other pages, open WooCommerce -> Settings -> Order.

Create the product pages for your WooCommerce site

The design of your product pages depends a lot on the theme used. It is in the menu Items ==> Add that you must go to edit your different product pages. WooCommerce allows you to create very comprehensive product pages, including all the necessary details about your products and their attributes. As we said previously, the editor is identical to the one used for classic WordPress sites (non-e-commerce).

You must, for each product page, define the title, write a description of the product, choose the category and tags (labels) to which the product is attached, add product images, etc. You can customize the URL path. Until then, editing a product page is done the same way as editing a blog post on WordPress. What changes is the "Product Data" block, which appears under the central part of the editor? This is also what makes one of the great strengths of WooCommerce. This block is used to manage all the elements specific to the product pages: price, delivery, stock status, dimensions and weight, options (color, size, etc.), complementary/similar products, etc. This block allows you to create very complete product pages giving all the information your customers need. We invite you to take a look at all the tabs in this block to familiarize yourself with and optimize your product pages.

You will find that creating a product page on WooCommerce is a snap. It will not take you long to get to grips with this editor. If you want to offer multiple products on your WooCommerce site (which it probably is!), You will need to organize these products into different categories. To do this, you must go to Products ==> Categories. What is very convenient, especially if you have a large catalog, is that you have the option of creating sub-categories. I want to emphasize in this guide the key points taken into account when creating a WooCommerce site: the first settings, the choice of the theme, the peculiarities of the product page editor, etc. We could have spent more time on certain technical points, such as setting the delivery options for example. But that would have unnecessarily lengthened this guide. To go further, we advise you to refer once again to the excellent documentation made available to you by WooCommerce.

Add Your First Product

For your online store to be truly operational, you will need products or services to sell! To add a new product, go to your WordPress console and click on "Products -> Add a product".

1. The name of your product

2. The general description of your product. This section allows you to add a lot of text content. Using the WYSIWYG tools, you will even be able to add images, videos, tables, titles, etc.

3. The portion of the data relating to your product. Use this to first indicate whether your product is a physical, virtual, or downloadable product. If this is a physical product, do not check a box. If it is a service, it is considered a virtual product. Here are the other portions of this central section:

- General: Which is used to define the price of the product and its taxes
- Inventory: To manage your inventory (if necessary)
- Shipping: To define the dimensions, weight and delivery price of the product
- Related products: To define similar products like: "Customers who bought this product also bought these..."
- Attributes: To add attributes such as size, color, material, etc.
- Advanced: Containing the fields "Purchase note", "Menu order" and "Activate reviews"

4. Short Product Description: This text will be displayed under the product title in the (single-product) product page.

5. Product categories: To group products from the same category (e.g.: "sweaters" category under the "men" category)

6. Product labels: Another way to group your products (ex: specific brands)

7. Product image: The main image of your product (which will also be used in miniature in your category pages or on the Shop page)

8. Product gallery: A gallery containing different images of your product

Chapter Five

Designing E-Commerce Webpages with Elementor and the Design of other Sections

Elementor is a visual page builder that offers the 'Drag and Drop' feature that allows you to easily create custom layouts on WordPress without any coding knowledge. In this section, we'll show you how to easily create custom WordPress layouts with Elementor with just a few clicks.

Why and when to create custom layouts in WordPress?

Many free and premium WordPress themes offer multiple layout choices for different types of pages. However, sometimes none of these layout templates meet your needs. However, if you are keen on PHP, HTML, and CSS, you have the option of creating your page templates or even creating a child theme for your website. But, the majority of WordPress users are not developers, so this option doesn't work for them.

So it would be great to create layouts using a simple interface (Drag and Drop). This is exactly what Elementor does. This is a WordPress page builder plugin that allows you to easily create your custom WordPress layouts without any coding skills. It has an intuitive user interface that allows you to create custom layouts with real-time preview. It comes with plenty of ready-made modules for all types of web design elements. It offers several professionally designed page templates that you can load and use instantly as a starting point. With that said, let's take a look at how to create custom WordPress layouts with the WordPress Elementor plugin.

Getting Started with Elementor

First, you will need to purchase the " Elementor Pro " plugin. This is the paid version of the free "Elementor" plugin that gives you access to additional features and 1 year of customer support.

Secondly, you will need to install and activate the Elementor plugin. You can refer to the previous section on how to install a WordPress plugin. After activation, visit the " Elementor> Settings" page to configure how this plugin works.

Here you can activate "Elementor" for different post types. By default, it is enabled for your WordPress posts and pages. If you have custom post formats on your website, those will also appear here, and you can enable them as well. You will be able to exclude or include user roles that can use Elementor while writing posts or pages. By default, it is enabled only for administrators. Remember to click on the "Save Changes" button to save your settings.

Creating a custom layout with Elementor

First, you need to create a new page (or post) on your WordPress website. On the post edit page, you will notice the new "Edit With Elementor" button.

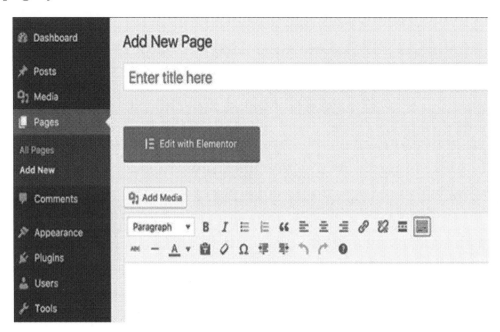

Clicking on it will launch the Elementor user interface where you can edit your page using the visual page builder with drag and drop functionality.

You can now add sections and build your page from scratch, or you can still load one of the default templates. Templates are a faster way to get started quickly. Thus, Elementor offers several professionally designed templates that you can customize as much as you want. Let's start with a model by clicking on the "Add a model" button. This will bring up a pop-up window where you can see the different models available. You should look for a model that looks like what you want.

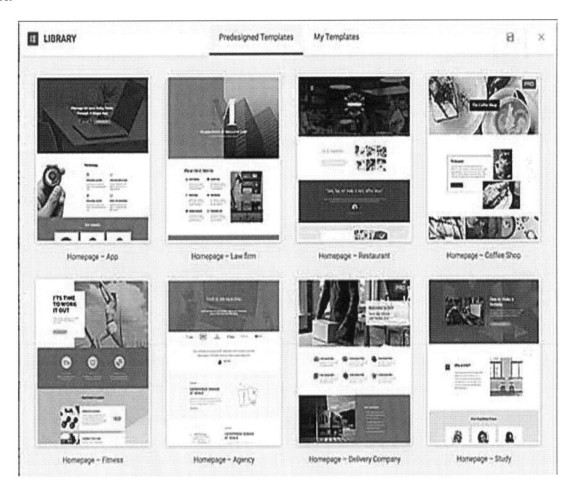

Now click to select the template you want and then click on the "Insert" button to add it to your page. Elementor will load the template for you.

You can now start modifying the template to suit your needs. Just point and click on any element to select it, and Elementor will show you its settings in the left column.

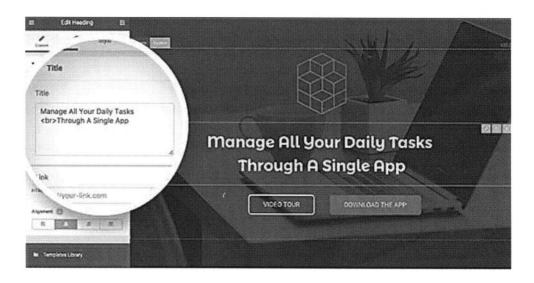

Now let's talk about how Elementor's layouts work. The templates offered by the Elementor plugin are built on sections, columns, and widgets. Sections are like lines or blocks that you place on your page. Each section can have multiple columns and each section and column can have its styles, colors, content, etc.

You have the option of adding elements to your columns and sections using the widgets that Elementor offers. These widgets are types of content blocks that you can place in sections of your pages. Just select a widget and drop it in your section or column. There is a huge set of widgets available that cover every popular web design element you can imagine.

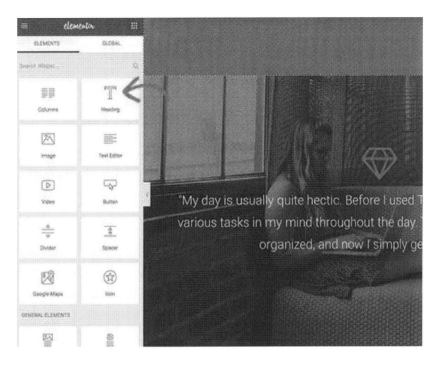

You can add images, texts, topics, image galleries, videos, maps, icons, testimonials, sliders, carousels, and much more. You can also add default WordPress widgets and even widgets created by other WordPress plugins to your website. Once you are done creating your or modifying your layout, you can click on the " Save " button to keep your changes.

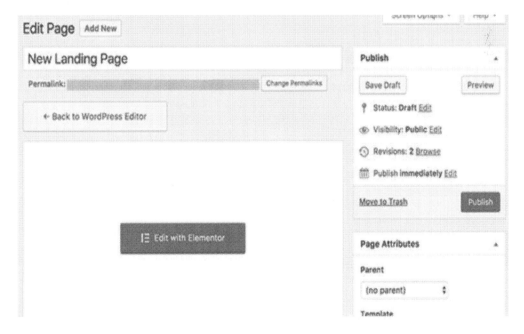

Note: Saving a layout will not publish the page to your WordPress website. It will simply save your layout. At this point, you have the option to preview your page or go to the WordPress dashboard. Which will bring you back to the default WordPress post editor. You can now save your WordPress page or publish it to your website. That's it, so finished creating a page with the WordPress Elementor plugin. But like many visual page builders, it also offers extensions that will allow you to easily and quickly create new layouts by bringing more design elements to the default plugin.

Chapter Six

How to Market and Promote your E-Commerce Store

Build an SEO friendly E-commerce Site to gain Online presence

Something promised, something due. After having explained the methodology to pre-launch your online store, we will focus in particular on SEO preparation. I'll show you a technique that will save you time and not start from scratch. The first step is to determine the keywords that are important to your store. Got your keyword list to work on in SEO? Very well. Let's move on. To make this clearer, I will use an example. Your future store will sell shirts for men. During your keyword research, you noticed that the keyword "men's black shirt" was interesting. So you want your future store to have a good position on this query (I remind you that this is an example, nothing says that this keyword is interesting). The technique is to create on your pre-launch site (blog or mini-site, it doesn't matter) a content page optimized for the query "black shirt for men."

Concretely, this page will have the URL and its on-page elements will be optimized for this request: title tag, h1, and h2 tags highlighting of the keyword (in bold, in italics), use of variants to widen the lexical field, etc... This page should be rich in content. Aim for a page of at least 1000 words (I admit, writing a 1000 word page on men's black shirts is not easy!). Ok, this page is live. Google will, therefore, be able to visit it and index it in its database (you can use the Google Webmaster Tool for faster indexing). By the time your online store is ready, this page will have had a little history.

But that's not all. Since this page is live, you can arrange to have links that point to this page. The backlinks being a very important criterion for Google, it will be able to help to make climb this page (of course, provided you do it right). In fact, on the day you launch your E-commerce, the page of your store that will showcase all black shirts for men will come over the optimized page. That is to say that on the URL you will no longer have your page of at least 1000 words but you will have a page listing all the models of black shirts for men.

If you can successfully position the "/black-shirt-man" content page on Google, you will get hits from that keyword. The day this content page is overwritten by its "online store" version, visitors will immediately see the page with all the men's black shirts, which may bring you sales. This technique is not miraculous either. Indeed, for its effects to be felt, two conditions are necessary:

1. Do it on a certain number of queries (if you want to work on 20 keywords, you will need to create 20 optimized pages)

2. Hope that Google does not lower the position of your page, once it has switched to online store mode (because it will certainly be less optimized than the "content" version)

This technique is a bit far-fetched, but it is not prohibited (you have the right to change the content of a page). In the past, I had the opportunity to test this technique, with interesting results (on the day of the launch of the online store, there were over 500 visitors from Google). However, not having tested it on many sites, I, unfortunately, cannot say that it works every time.

As you have seen, you don't have to wait until the day you launch your online store to worry about its marketing. You can (and should) think about it long before it goes live. I have endeavored to present you techniques that are easy to implement and inexpensive or inexpensive. "Only" your time will have to be used (which is not bad enough, I admit). Don't see this work as a waste of time, but for what it is: a way for your site to be successful... right from the start!

Paid SEO: Online advertising for your e-commerce site

Paid SEO (or SEA for Search Engine Advertising) corresponds to online advertising. For e-merchants, advertising online brings immediate visibility to its online store. There are several platforms for advertising on the internet, but for e-commerce, we recommend the Google Ads platform. This advertising platform belonging to the internet giant offers you:

- Budget control and real monitoring of results (no budget overruns and exact monitoring of costs).
- Precise conversion tracking (you know exactly which keywords, which ads have led to a conversion)
- A real compliment to SEO (some queries are very competitive and it is sometimes difficult to reach the top spots in the SERP, while with paid SEO you can get ahead of your competitors by being visible above the natural results).

If you choose Google Ads, we can only encourage you to use Google Shopping. It is thanks to this tool that advertisements showing products with an image, a price, and a link to the merchant site are published when you search on Google.

There is nothing more efficient if you have an online store. The great advantage of Shopping ads is indeed their high visibility:

- Shopping ads can be found on Google but also Youtube, Google Images and many other partner sites
- The presence of a visual accompanied by the price and availability makes it easier to click
- The conversion rate of Shopping ads is very good.

While Shopping comes highly recommended, don't limit yourself to just one type of ad. Google Ads offers many other types of advertisements that help promote your products and services, or simply promote your brand:

The ads Search are advertisements in text only, which is found in the very first results of the SERP. They are useful for targeting people looking for a specific product or service on the net (eg: "Alsace web agency", "Alsace e-commerce site creation"). It can also be used to highlight promotions.

The Display ads are graphical ads that are seen on other websites (not in the SERP). They make it possible to promote a product or present a promotion based on precise targeting. Display ads are also ideal for remarketing: they are ads that only offer ads related to products that Internet users have already viewed on your site.

The mobile ads: smartphones are fast becoming the No. 1 unit to browse the web; it would be dangerous to ignore advertisements to this medium. Google Ads allows you to create mobile-friendly advertising ads, with very practical features for this medium (e.g. "Call only" ads allow Internet users pressing your ad to call you directly with their fingertips, without even dialling your number. phone).

The impact of Social Media Sites on Promotion of Online Stores

Social networks are an effective channel to market your product and your company. You can post product photos on your Instagram, Pinterest, or Facebook profiles and even make presentation videos on Youtube. With a little originality and staging, you spark the interest of your audience and make sales or gain popularity. For example, contests and promotions are very good ways to create interactions with Internet users on social networks.

But social networks, like Google, have also developed their advertising services. For example, you can create advertising posts on Facebook (Facebook Ads) to reach personalized audiences. As with Google Ads Displays, these are promotional visuals broadcast on the news feed of Facebook users according to the criteria you define (audience, budget, location (Facebook, Instagram, Messenger, Audience Network), ad format).

But you can also use social networks as a real online catalog of products by:

- Adding a store to your Facebook page: This feature allows you to create a product catalog (with a visual and a price for each product) which links to your merchant site to finalize the order.
- Using the Shop the Look Pins on Pinterest or the Shopping in Instagram feature: these tools allow certain merchants (ready-to-wear, decoration, etc.) to have their products identified on publications (with price display).

78

The Internet user who has a crush on a product presented in a post can be redirected directly to your online store to finalize his purchase.

You will understand, there are many techniques to promote your e-commerce site. To properly invest your time and money to obtain real results, the best thing is to seek advice from web marketing professionals.

How to Advertise your E-Commerce Site with Google Shopping (Google Ads)

Google ads are a price comparison service making it possible to strengthen the visibility of the product catalog of e-merchants in Google. Google Shopping was launched in 2010 in the USA before being rolled out in many other countries. This service is an almost essential acquisition channel if you are an e-merchant, even if it has been paid for since 2012. Well used, Google Shopping can help you boost your sales and your turnover. But how do you set up and use Google Shopping correctly? After reviewing what Google Shopping consists of (operation and history), we offer a complete tutorial from creating your Google Merchant Center account to designing your Google Shopping campaign from Google AdWords.

Google Shopping, what is it for?

Google Shopping is a Google service accessible directly from the search engine. It is a sort of search engine for physical products, quite similar in its operation to a comparator of products and prices. A Google Shopping block appears directly in Google search results for e-commerce type queries such as "running sports shoes." On some requests, the Google Shopping block can be moved to the right-sidebar, jostled by Google AdWords ads and possibly the Google MyBusiness block. By clicking on the "Shopping" tab, you access the complete comparison, with filtering options and the list of all the products associated with the query

The Internet user can filter the results using many criteria: new / used, price, category, color, gender (men/women), merchants (decathlon.fr, priceminister.com, etc.). If you are an e-merchant, being present in Google Shopping allows you to potentially significantly increase the visibility of your products and ultimately increase your turnover. Unlike Adwords ads, Shopping "ads" provide very detailed information on a particular product: the name of the product, a description, the price of the product, the price of delivery, any promotions, customer reviews, etc. Not to mention the image which considerably enriches the ads.

This level of precision allows you to bring much more qualified than average traffic to your e-commerce site. A user who clicks on a Google Shopping link is much more likely to convert (and buy a product) than a user who clicks on a text-only link (natural or Adwords) in search results. Google Shopping makes it possible to profit more effectively from the Google audience when you are an e-merchant and sell physical products. Google Shopping is a very interesting channel and more and more used by e-merchants. Note that Google Shopping results also appear on mobile (the opposite would have been surprising). By clicking on "See the offer" in the ad, the Internet user is automatically redirected to your e-commerce site. Google Shopping offers a much more suitable display for physical product ads than AdWords ads.

Tip: Promoting visuals is one of the great features of Google Shopping. To make Internet users want to click on your ads, take good care of your product images (centered photos, HD, and white backgrounds preferably). Before explaining to you how to make your products appear on Google Shopping, let's quickly go back to the origin of this service, which has undergone several changes.

A brief history of the service, from Product Search to Google Shopping

Google Shopping was born in 2010. It is the successor of the Froogle service, renamed Google Product Search from 2007. The main characteristic of Google Product Search, which differentiated it at the time from other comparators, was that it was free. GPS was completely free. Google Shopping replaced Google Product Search in 2010. Google Shopping became chargeable from 2012. Search results in Google Shopping are now both determined based on relevance criteria (including taking into account descriptions, titles, technical data, images, customer reviews) and by the amount paid by e-merchants. Google Shopping uses the same system as Adwords (auctions + CPC). We will also see that the configuration of Google Shopping campaigns is done from the AdWords interface.

Like AdWords, Google Shopping uses:

An auction system. The one with the highest bid appears first in the results.

A CPC model (cost per click). As a Google Shopping user, you are billed by Google each time an Internet user clicks on your ad (on "See offer"). You can set a daily budget that should not be exceeded. Signing up to the Google Merchant Center and simply viewing your products on the Shopping platform is free.

Google Shopping was launched initially in the United States and the United Kingdom, then in Germany. It is now deployed in a very large number of countries.

How does Google Shopping work?

To fully understand how Google Shopping works, you have to understand the link between Google's three services, Google Shopping, Google Merchant Center, and Google Adwords. You might think that creating a Google Shopping campaign involves opening a "Google Shopping" account. However, this is not at all how Google Shopping works. There is no Google Shopping account. Google Shopping is simply the name of the storefront, of Google's eCommerce comparator whose history we have just recalled. To create a Google Shopping campaign, you must create a Merchant Center account and link this account to your Adwords account(if you don't have one, you will need to create one). Merchant Center and AdWords constitute, in a way, the back office of Google Shopping.

Google Merchant Center is the platform that allows you to send all the information about your products to Google. The first step when you want to get started in Google Shopping is to upload your product catalog (in table form) to Google Merchant Center. For Google to be able to show your products in search results and the Shopping tab, it must first have all the information about your catalog (price, delivery, product characteristics, etc.). We will explain in detail how to do this in the next paragraph. It is from the Merchant Center interface that you can update your catalog at any time (add new products, modify prices, etc.).

Google AdWords, which you probably already know, is the platform that allows you to create your Google Shopping campaigns. Google's Shopping ads are a form of advertising. Who says advertising on Google, says Google AdWords. We can say, without departing from reality, that Google Shopping is only a particular display mode of AdWords ads. As we have seen, the economic model is the same: the CPC (you pay when the Internet user clicks on the ad). You can set the daily budget and CPC for your Google Shopping campaign from AdWords.

To see more clearly, here are all the steps to follow to create a Google Shopping campaign:

- Create an account on Google Merchant Center.
- Configure this account and prove that you are the owner of your e-commerce site. This is the site validation/claim step. It can be done in several ways, including linking your Google Merchant Center account to your Google Search Console account.
- Import your product catalog into Google Merchant Center, creating a table (rows for products, columns for attributes) and then creating a data feed.
- Create your Google Shopping campaign on AdWords.

Creating an account on Google Merchant Center

Creating an account on Google Merchant Center is very easy and will only take you a few minutes. As with all other Google services, you must have a Google account to register with Merchant Center. If you use a Gmail or Google Analytics box, you must have one. If you don't have one, start by creating one for yourself. It'll take you two-three minutes. If you already have a Google address or have just created it, go to the Google Merchant Center site at this address. Click on "Register" at the top right of the screen. Google can ask you for information: location of your activity, name of your store/company, URL of your e-commerce site (with HTTP:// or https: // in front), main contact.

Once you have entered this information, go to the next step. Google asks you to accept the terms of service. Do this before taking the last step. In this last step, Google asks you to validate and claim your site. This is for Google to ensure that you are the owner of the site and to authorize Google to use the data on your site. To do this, you need to copy and paste your URL into the specified field. There are then several methods of proving that you are the owner of the site. The easiest method is to upload an HTML file to your site's server. You will need to leave this HTML file on your server to maintain owner status.

There are other ways to verify and claim your website. Here they are:

- The "HTML tag" method, which consists of adding a Meta tag to your home page. This supposes being able to modify the HTML source code of the index page. As with the HTML file, the meta tag should not be deleted once your site has been validated.
- The "Google Analytics" method. If you are already using Google Analytics to analyze your e-commerce site statistics, simply copy and paste the asynchronous Google Analytics tracking code into the header of your site.
- The "Google Tag Manager" method. If you use this server, just add the GTM container extract to your website.

There is one last method. If you've already validated your URL in Google Search Console, just add the Google account you use for Merchant Center as the Search Console account owner. If you are using the same Google Account for Merchant Center and Search Console, you do not need to go through the "validation" step. Your site is already validated. So just claim the URL from the "Website verification" tab. Validating your site consists of proving that you are the owner. Claiming your site involves linking your site to Google Merchant Center and enabling data transfers.

Note: You can skip the verify/claim step and do it later. You will then have to go to the Google Merchant Center interface in Settings> Website verification. Regardless, we recommend that you verify and claim your site right away, especially if you're planning to start a Google Shopping campaign right away.

Once these steps are completed, you are redirected to the Google Merchant Center interface. You must now enter information about you and your company in the "Settings" menu. In particular, you are invited to indicate your delivery methods and to configure the taxes (amount of VAT). Complete your account information as much as possible.

Link your e-commerce site to Google Merchant Center: Create a product feed.

Now that you have created and configured your Google Merchant Center account, you need to import all the products in your catalog that you want to be displayed on the Google Shopping platform. Let's say it right away: this is the most complex and longest step. For this, you need to create a product feed. A product feed is a tabular file that summarizes all the information about the products you want to appear on Google Shopping. Each row corresponds to a product, and each column an attribute (product name, price, color, etc.). To create this file, you have several solutions. You can import a table in.xml or.txt format, or you can use Google Sheets.

Some of the attributes in your product table are required, some are optional. The attributes will be used in the display of your products on Google Shopping. Using optional attributes will allow you to enrich the information that will appear in Google Shopping. Here is the list of mandatory attributes for all products:

The identifier: It must be unique for each product. If you use multiple product feeds, you cannot reuse the same ID in your different files. Most e-merchants use the article code to define the identifier.

The title: This is the name or designation of the article. The title appears in Google Search or Google Shopping results. The title should be explicit, meaningful. It is possible to mention in the title the size, color, or other important characteristics attached to the article. On the other hand, it is not possible to integrate promotional messages in the title.

Description: This is a very important element, for the Internet user of course, but also by Google, which will analyze its content to display the results. It plays an essential role in the referencing of your products in Google Shopping. Think about SEO optimization (keywords, etc.). You are limited to 5,000 characters.

The link: This is the landing page to which Google will refer if the Internet user clicks on "See the offer". You can configure this URL to be able to track it later on Google Analytics.

Image link: This is the URL of the main image. Note that you can also add secondary images. For the main image, choose good quality photos with optimized weight.

Condition: This is to indicate whether your product is new, used, or reconditioned.

Availability: This involves specifying whether the product is in stock, not available, or on pre-order.

The price. Remember to respect Google's nomenclature: "20.45 USD".

The brand: If you are a reseller, you must indicate the name of the brand of the product and not the name of your resale company.

The Gtin: This is the barcode of your product. In Europe, the EAN code (GTIN-13), 13 digits are used.

The manufacturer reference, allowing the manufacturer to be identified.

The category: be careful, these are not your product categories but those used by Google. You cannot choose two categories for the same product.

Delivery: you must indicate in this field the number of shipping costs and the type of delivery.

The easiest way to create your product table is to use a Google Sheets spreadsheet (Google's online software very similar to Excel). By using Google Sheets, Google provides you with file templates that will save you a lot of time (by clicking on "Add-ons"). You can also use Excel, but you will need to save your table in.txt format because Merchant Center does not recognize Excel (.xls) format.

Your product feed will need to be regularly updated in the event of price changes, changes in delivery, change in availability, new product, etc. Moreover, your feed remains active for a month. If you don't do any updates for a month, Google will send you an email asking you to do so. You should, therefore, do at least one update per month. Note that Bigcommerce allows you to directly import your catalog and automatically update your product file. If you are using Prestashop, Magento, or WooCommerce, be aware that plugins are allowing you to do the same. Type "Google Merchant Center" in your CMS app/plugin store. Some plugins/extensions are free, others pay.

Add a feed on Google Merchant Center:

When you add a product feed to Google Merchant Center, Google will ask you for several pieces of information (see screenshot below). Here are some details on the subject:

- **Mode:** You have the choice between "Standard" and "Test". The "Test" mode allows you to check that your feed contains no errors before displaying your products on Google Shopping. The "Standard" mode will allow Google to display the products contained in your feed on Google Shopping.
- **Type of feed:** Select "Products".

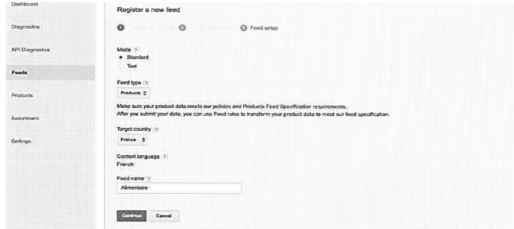

- **Target Country:** Indicates the country in which your Google Shopping ads will appear. If you choose France, your descriptions must be in French and you must use the euro as the currency (logical...).
- **Content Language:** This is the language used in your product file.
- **Feed name:** As the name suggests, this is about giving your feed a name. This will help you find your way around if you are using multiple feeds.

Once your feed is registered, you can follow the import status of your products from the "Products" tab of the interface. In the event of problems encountered importing your product catalog, go to the "Diagnosis" tab. Forgetting mandatory attributes is a frequent source of errors.

Note: As you may have noticed, you can create multiple product feeds. This is particularly interesting if you want to promote your products on Google Shopping in several countries. Each flow will correspond to a specific target country (and a specific currency if applicable).

Link Google Merchant Center to AdWords

Once you've created your product feed, you'll need to link your Google Merchant Center account to AdWords to create your Google Shopping campaign. This step (and the next) has become mandatory since the Google Shopping storefront is paying. Linking Google Merchant Center to AdWords allows you to transmit to your AdWords account the data contained in your Merchant Center account (= your product feed). The principle is simple: you will have to send a request to link Merchant Center to AdWords from your Merchant Center account. Then you need to go to your AdWords account to accept the request. Which assumes that you own both accounts.

To send the request from Google Merchant Center, go to Settings> AdWords. If you are using the same account to manage Merchant Center and AdWords, click "Create an account". If you are using two different Google Accounts for Merchant Center and AdWords, click "Link another account". In the latter case, you must enter the AdWords customer number which is displayed at the top right of the screen when you are on AdWords.

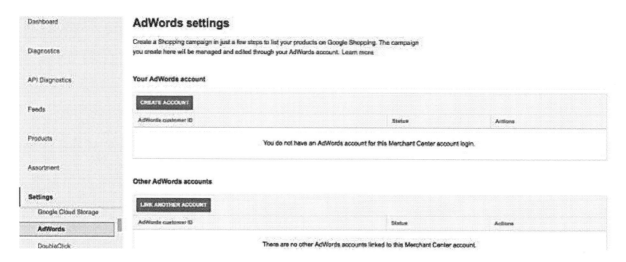

You must then go to your AdWords account in Settings> Linked accounts to accept the link request. Click on "View the request" then on "Approve." Data relating to your products imported to the Merchant Center is now available on AdWords. Note: You can optionally link multiple AdWords accounts to the same Merchant Center account. Or the other way around: link several Merchant Center accounts to your AdWords account. You can now create your Google Shopping campaign.

Creating ads on AdWords and set the budget

We will quickly go over this last step. Creating a Google Shopping campaign is not much different than creating a regular AdWords campaign. In particular, you must choose a CPC and set a daily budget. To create your first Google Shopping campaign, click on "+ Campaign" in the Campaign menu. A drop-down menu appears. Choose "Shopping."

On the "Select Campaign Parameters" page, you must name your campaign, select the "merchant referral" and choose a country of sale. By choosing "France" as the country of sale, the Shopping campaign will concern all the products of the Merchant Center flows for which you have chosen France as the target country. The "merchant reference" means the identifier of your Merchant Center account. Remember to fill in as much information as possible on this page to personalize your campaigns. In particular, you can determine the priority of your Google Shopping campaign by clicking on Shopping settings (advanced). This is useful if you run multiple Shopping campaigns (with different bids) promoting the same

88

product. By default, all Shopping campaigns are assigned a "low" priority by Google. More interestingly, you can filter the products affected by your Google Shopping campaign. Each filter (or condition) corresponds to a specific attribute in your product feed. In the example below, we want to set up a campaign to promote our Sony electronics only. You can choose up to 7 different filters.

At the very bottom of the page, you are prompted to set the maximum CPC and your daily budget. As was recalled at the beginning, you are billed at CPC, that is, per click (CPC = cost per click). The higher you set a maximum CPC, the better you'll rank in Google Shopping. Google highlights the ads that offer the highest bid. The daily budget, as the name suggests, is the amount that you are willing to spend on average each day. Your ads will appear for the day as soon as your daily budget is met. These two criteria - CPC and daily budget - can be changed at any time. Once you have filled in all the information, go to the next step: creating your ad groups. Ad groups allow you to assign specific auction rules to one or more product groups. To learn more, see our article on Google Adwords.

Creating your first Google Shopping campaign might seem a bit overwhelming. But once you've created your first product feed and familiarize yourself with how AdWords works (if you haven't already), you'll see that everything will go a lot faster. Google Shopping campaigns are an opportunity if you market physical products and plan to promote them on Google.

How to Advertise your E-commerce site on Facebook

Social media marketing has become essential for companies wishing to attract new customers on the web. Facebook, in particular, is a powerful social network for finding prospects. But how do you best use it as an e-merchant? The answer in 5 steps.

1) Choose the right Facebook page template

For some time now, Facebook has offered several predefined page templates: choosing an appropriate template is a first step in optimizing a page.

By default, your page follows the "Standard" template, but you can easily change this by going to Settings> Edit Page:

You then access a multitude of options:

- Business ;
- Places ;
- Non-profit organization;
- Politicians;
- Services ;
- Restaurants and cafes;
- Shopping.

The Shopping model is without hesitation the most suitable for an e-commerce activity since it facilitates the presentation of products and online shopping. It notably contains a "Shop" section allowing you to display your products.

2) Choose a good call-to-action

Your Facebook page has several buttons (under the cover photo). Among them, the most important is certainly the call-to-action represented by a big blue button. To maximize its effectiveness, it is essential to choose a relevant CTA. To do this, click on your button to access the list of possible options:

For an online sales activity, the "Buy or donate" category is the most interesting. Thus, you can very simply encourage your fans to buy your products or view your offers.

3) Create a Shop

By choosing the Shopping page template, you will have access to a "Shop" tab which will occupy a central place. You will need to adjust a few settings first: in particular, you can choose to redirect your customers to your site when they click on a product or allow them to buy directly from Facebook.

You can then describe what you are selling and add your products by filling in for each:

- A name ;
- A description ;
- A price ;
- A URL;
- Pictures.
- Result: your Facebook page turns into a real e-commerce mini-site.

4) Identify your products on your photos

Having products in stock in your store is a great start, but promoting them is even more important. To do this, there is an extremely useful feature: tagging products in your photos. As long as you have a shop tab containing products, you will have access to all your photos (including your cover photo) to an "Identify products" button. Very practical for promoting the goods you sell at a lower cost.

5) Activate customer reviews

If Internet users are often suspicious of brands, they trust the opinions of their peers much more: this is why customer reviews are essential to encourage your visitors to buy your products. That's great, with the Shopping template your Facebook page can have a Reviews tab to collect ratings and comments from your customers. Just make sure this feature is enabled in Settings> Edit page> Reviews.

Of course, this tactic is a double-edged sword: if you receive a lot of negative reviews, its impact will be rather harmful. Even more reason to guarantee a good quality of service to satisfy your customers and thus receive positive opinions!

Advertising your Store through Radio and Television Channels

- Television Advertising

Using TV advertising as a marketing plan offers a lot of benefits to a business. Indeed, this method makes it possible to obtain a major exposure towards the customers. But also, to increase the company's turnover and improve the gain in credibility. It is therefore important to know that TV advertising is one of the most powerful forms of communication. Studies have even shown that television is among the most dominant media in most households for developed countries.

TV advertising allows targets to have a sense of direct connection with the company. This is because potential customers have the chance to see and hear the prospecting without having to imagine them. It remains to plan a good spot that attracts the attention of spectators and makes it easier to memorize important information. For this, you have to prepare a spot including animations that are original and attractive. This will keep the spectators' attention and encourage them not to zap. TV commercials have several advantages for the development of a business. With the mastery of clubbing, it is quite possible to reach as many audiences as possible in a given period. This technique, therefore, remains very effective in making prospects aware of imminent events. The TV ad will increase the reputation of a company and improve its sales figures by displaying a single image on the screen. Also, it is easier to grab the attention of viewers with engaging, compelling, and fun content. Moreover, TV advertising also facilitates the promotion of products or services to customers. She provides as much information as possible on the subject. Any business that opts for a TV advertising strategy can expect to see its sales figures and brand awareness soar within three to four weeks of prospecting. Note that the stronger the reputation of the company at the outset, the faster the expected effects are revealed.

Television is a very free broadcasting medium. It allows all types of messages to be transmitted, ranging from a fixed sign, a photograph to a complex animation. To succeed in prospecting via television, it is advisable to follow the evolution of the public. And adapt the information disseminated to it to optimize its prospecting efficiency. Note that the influence of the public is so strong that it forbids laying down the rules for the manufacture of the advertisement itself.

The key to a successful TV advertising campaign is to stand out from the competition and boost the profile of the business to be promoted spectacularly. To do this, it is recommended to adapt the advertising spot according to the targeted prospects. For example, for seniors, we should opt for afternoon shows, for children, there are youth boxes, for professionals, there are specialized news channels.

- Radio Advertising

Communicating on local radios has become essential when it comes to reaching your consumers. It is nevertheless a question of using it well and finding the right time to launch a communication campaign. Radio reaches more than 8 out of 10 US people. To begin with, you should know that radio is a powerful medium. Here are some significant data:

- 82% of American people listen to it every day;

- Radio is their second most consumed medium, after television;

- It affects all populations, all age groups, and all socio-professional categories;

- The radio is what we call a proximity media, even of intimacy; we listen to the radio in our bedroom, in our car, in our bathroom...

- Their peak hours (the radio counts about 27 million listeners between 7 a.m. and 9 a.m.) before the store opens. When you ask a buyer about the last media seen before a purchase, 57% are radio!

Launching an advertising campaign and communicating on local radio stations will allow you to reach consumers located in your catchment area. Such a campaign is thus particularly indicated during events - in the broad sense - in your point of sale: opening, reopening after works, clearance sale, wine fair, sales. Your communication will resonate differently in the minds of your customers: for example, hearing that a supermarket offers -30% on school supplies is much more engaging for consumers when they hear a known address. Concrete, identifiable, the information "makes you want" to go to the point of sale. Especially since with local radio there is a phenomenon of appropriation on the part of listeners/consumers: they appreciate the dimension anchored in their daily lives. of the media, and lend a more attentive ear to the information disseminated... as to the advertisements! However, you must first ensure that there is consistency between the coverage area of the radio (s) selected and your catchment area, to reach the right people.

Here are some essential rules for an effective campaign:

- Invest in sound creation and choose a warm and friendly voice, suited to the message you want to convey;

- Prefer a short spot, generally 20 seconds;

- Focus your message on the event (promotion, opening or reopening of a store, the start of sales, promotional offers or commercial offers, etc.) with the emphasis on impactful terms, and not on the brand or sign;

- Remember to mention the exact address of your brand;

- Just as your establishment or brand has a logo, create your own sound identity;